Fannie Brooks James

Divine Science

New light upon old truths, to all who seek more light

Fannie Brooks James

Divine Science
New light upon old truths, to all who seek more light

ISBN/EAN: 9783337034443

Printed in Europe, USA, Canada, Australia, Japan

Cover: Foto ©Thomas Meinert / pixelio.de

More available books at **www.hansebooks.com**

DIVINE SCIENCE,

New Light Upon Old Truths.

·

TO ALL WHO SEEK MORE LIGHT.

"SEEK AND YE SHALL FIND."

MRS. FANNIE B. JAMES.

DENVER, COLORADO:
BARKHAUSEN & LESTER, PRINTERS,
1896.

IMPORTANT TO ALL READERS.

As the lessons in this book are designed to be studies upon the Science, or right knowledge of Divinity, the subject is taken from its starting point in the Divine, and step by step is it developed from the Source and Cause of all things.

Therefore each study makes that which follows it plain, and it is decidedly important that the lessons be read, or *studied* rather, in their order.

To one who has never had opportunity to study this truly Divine Science, we would suggest that they may find, by careful thought, a complete understanding of the principle and practice of the Science of Life, in these lessons.

So we advise such, to lay aside questions at first; read each lesson to gain clearly the point considered in it; let all else alone. Read one lesson each day, or even on alternate days; reread often, until the subject of it is understood, before studying the next. By so doing, without a teacher, the knowledge of the Science may be gained, and its practice understood.

INTRODUCTORY THOUGHTS.

THE KINGDOM OF HEAVEN.

The WORDS of Jesus the Christ are growing in significance—or, are coming to us with deeper *meaning* to-day than in any age before this. One minister has said, "The Bible means more to us than it did to our parents; it will mean more to our children than it does to us." Another said, "The sunday school children of to-day are better able to understand Jesus' teachings than were the disciples of old."

Jesus said to his disciples, "I have *many things* to say unto you, but *ye* cannot *bear them now*"; which plainly shows us that Jesus was limited in his speaking of the Truth, by the dulness of his hearers. He could give to the disciples only what they were able to "bear," or to receive. He sometimes rebuked their lack of understanding.—*Matt. 15:16; Mark 8:21.*

From His words quoted, and those which followed—"Howbeit, when He, the Spirit of Truth, is come, he will guide you into *all* Truth"—we may conclude that Jesus had a reserve of Truth, which he would gladly have expressed, but that it could not be understood even by the disciples; and that he knew and foretold in these words, how the revelation of fuller Truth would *continue* from

2004005

the Spirit throughout the ages to come, until " all Truth"
had been received and understood.

This certainly contradicts our past ignorant belief,
that all revelation ceased with the "good old times";
and that the " voice from heaven " has long been silent—
it can speak to us no more ! Is revelation finished ?

The Truth will never cease to speak within our souls,
while there is anything of God not comprehended.
" Take heed how ye *hear.*"—*Luke 8:18.*

"There is nothing covered that shall not be revealed. "—*Matt. 10:26.* Revelation cannot be finished
until every mystery is made plain: revelation is not
therefore limited to any time or place; and whenever or
wherever there is the spirit to receive and be taught,
fuller and higher Truth is being made known.

One says, " Revelation is unveiling; but the veil is
on the face of man and not on the face of God. " The
" veil " is a fitting symbol of our own ignorance; with
every new revelation of Truth the " veil " grows thinner.
" Which veil is done away in Christ. "—*2 Cor. 3:14-16.*

Christ is " The way, the truth and the life. " As fast
as we are able to be led in the " Way, " and to "bear, "
or carry in our hearts the " Truth, " and to "hear, " or
understand the so-called " mysteries " of " Life, " just so
surely is the " veil, " or lack of understanding, being
" done away. "

"Clouds and darkness are round about Him, " is
David's conception of God, and with Jeremiah we have
been willing to say, " Thou hast covered thyself with a
cloud, that our prayer should not pass through. "—*Lam.
3:44.* But we may rejoice in the increasing light, which
now reveals that around God are no impenetrable clouds !

As well might we say on a cloudy day, " The sun has
wrapped himself in clouds and darkness. " The clouds

that hide the sun from us, and shut out the warmth and brightness of its presence, are *around our earth*, and arise *from the earth*. These intercept the light of the sun, so that it does not reach us, but the sun shines on and on unaltered by the clouds around *us*.

So the clouds of darkness, fear, sorrow or doubt that seem to come into our lives, are around *us*, and not near the source of Light and Love. Neither do they come from the source of Love, but arise from our own incompleteness, or incomplete understanding.

As long as we see "clouds" about us, there is need of further revelation, or unveiling. As long as we have the Spirit of God, the Spirit of Wisdom, Truth and Love with us, we shall *still be taught of God*, and shall go on hearing Truth more and more clearly.

New things shall be revealed—must be—while the Spirit continues to lead us into all Truth. Revelation never ceases unless we close our eyes and ears to it.

Shall we then shrink from the " new," or shall we " Prove all things, holding fast that which is good " ?— *1 Thess. 5:21.*

Jesus said, " Ye shall know the truth, and the truth shall make you free. "—*Jno. 8:32.* These words express a truth for *all* times, as long as man any where is not free. The promise is given *to-day*, to every yearning one, who feels the depression of bondage to the flesh, or to " The ills that flesh is heir to. "

From these words we may gather three suggestions: First, that ignorance, or *not* knowing the truth, is the cause of our bondage ; second, that the relief from all bondage shall come through knowledge of truth ; and third, that we *shall* come into this knowledge and be made free. In this last is the promise of progression

and hint of continued revelation   How could we otherwise come to know all truth ?

Also in this is the blessed assurance that when we
have understanding of the truth as it is, we shall have
perfect freedom.   "Where the Spirit of the Lord is,
there is liberty."—*2 Cor. 3:17.*   "My people are destroyed for lack of knowledge."—*Hos. 4:6.*

What is this Truth that shall make us free, and
where is it to be found ?

Jesus declared, concerning his mission to earth, "To
this end was I born, and for this cause came I into the
world, that I should *bear witness* unto the *truth.*"—*Jno.
18:37.* Certainly this Divine One understood that the
need of man was to *know* the *Truth,* and announced himself as the teacher and living witness of Truth.

From Him them we may expect to catch the clear-
est idea of what and where Truth is.   We would not still
be asking these questions if man could have understood
his answer to them at that time. He said, "The kingdom of heaven is *at hand.*   The kingdom of God is *within you.*"—*Matt. 10:7.   Luke 7:21.*

If we are able now to "bear" these words, we shall
find in them no uncertain sound. The kingdom of God—
all that heaven is—the kingdom of Truth, of Love and of
Peace, is not afar off, but at hand, within us!

We have heeded these words so little, that our
heaven—our good and our peace "at hand," has been
literally *overlooked,* as we have tried to stretch our gaze
into the beyond. We have been taught to place our
happiness in the future, at some other time and place.
We have sung, " I'm but a pilgrim here, heaven is my
home." *We* have put off everything good to a future
heaven. How can we see and enter into "heaven" right

here and now, if we do not know the truth about it being at hand, and within us.

Like the patriarchs of old, we have "Died in the faith, not having received the promises, but having seen them afar off; and truly, if they had been mindful of that from whence they came out, they might have had opportunity to have returned."—*Heb. 11: 13-15.*

When shall we become "mindful?"—

When shall we accept our heaven? Not until we know the truth of it. "*Now* is the accepted time." Now is the time to accept—and there can never be any better opportunity than now, for it is all right here. "At hand." "Within you."

> "How far from here to heaven? Not very far, my friend;
> A single hearty step will all thy journey end.
> Hold, there! where runnest thou? Know heaven is in thee.
> Seekest thou for God elsewhere, His face thou'lt never see."

Is not our question answered? Where is the Truth? Everywhere! Heaven is the kingdom of Truth. Heaven is wherever God is. God is everywhere. Truth's "kingdom" is within us; is all around us. Our only need is to know the Truth, to have our eyes opened and our faces unveiled to see the everpresent goodness and Truth.

We remember the story of one who sought the temple of fame. He had been told-by those who had never been there to see, that it stood on the summit of a distant mountain. The youth left the plane of his every day life, forsook all else and spent the years of his life in toiling up the steep mountain in order to reach the temple. At last, aged and weary, he attained the height and looked eagerly for his treasure; he saw no temple, and, wandering on, he met an old man, who looked sadly at him, appreciating his earnest and worthy effort, but pitying his mistake, and said: "My friend, the temple you seek stands in the midst of the place you have left."

May we not expect something like this to greet us as we finish life's journey here, thinking to find our heaven at the end of our faithful toiling to attain it ? Shall we have to learn then instead of now, that our heaven is within us ?   If we listen to the voice of the one who knows, we will have no reason for any delusion. Heaven is now and always "within you—at hand." .

Heaven is God's presence, and God's presence is the Truth which we may know and accept at *this moment* as now and here; and knowing this Truth, shall make us free.

Truth never changes; it is "The same yesterday, to-day and forever."   It fills the universe of God, hence all Truth is here and now, and all that is true is eternal.

There is no *new* Truth.   Man may gain new ideas of the Truth, and revelation of God must bring new ideas to us, but this does not alter one iota of the Eternal Truth.

Truth must contain many things *new to us*, and these new things must be among the "many things" that Jesus could not tell to his disciples, but promised that the Spirit should reveal them as soon as they could be received.

Why then be afraid of a new idea of Truth ?   Why hesitate to accept something that has not been "seen" or "heard" before by us ?   It is written, "Eye hath not seen, ear hath not heard, neither hath it entered into the heart of man, what God hath prepared."—*1 Cor. 2:9.* We have not yet conceived of the things that Truth hath in store for us; we never shall know if we refuse to accept a new idea.

This idea of progress in spiritual understanding, is clearly taught in the Bible. "Greater works shall he do" ("that believeth on me," which makes these words apply to believers of every age.) Paul speaks of "milk" for "babes," and "strong meat" for "full age." Simple spiritual thoughts for us in immature consciousness, but strong sustenance for fuller developed thought. "That we may *grow* up *into* Him in all things." "Till we all come * * to the measure of the fulness of the stature of Christ."—*Eph. 4:13.* "Therefore *leaving* the principles (or first teachings) of the doctrine of Christ, let us *go on* to perfection."—*Heb. 6:1, 2.*

Truth is never afraid to declare new things. It says, *Isaiah 42:9,* "New things do I declare"; *43:19,* "Behold I will do a new thing"; *62:2,* "Thou shalt be called by new name"; *65:17,* "Behold I create a new heaven and a new earth"; *Ezek. 11:19,* "I will put a new spirit within you"; *Matt. 26:28,* "This is my blood of the new testament"; *Mark 16:17,* "They (that believe on Me) shall speak with new tongues"; *Jno. 13:34,* "A new commandment give I unto you"; *2 Cor. 5:17,* "If any man be *in* Christ (the Truth) he is a new creature, all things have become new"; *Col. 3:10,* "Put on the new man"; *Rev. 2:17,* "To him that overcometh will I give . . . a new name"; *3:12,* "I will write upon him my new name"; *5:9,* "They sung a new song"; *21:5,* "Behold I make *all things* new."

Why, we cannot enter into Truth until we are ready to accept all these "new" things. Truth is not changing. "New things" are only the eternal things *seen* by a new light—even by Divine illumination called the Spirit.

The church has always feared to entertain the idea

of progress in religion. The Jewish church is the first example of this. One says: "If Jesus had taught no higher truth than the Jews had received from their forefathers, they would have heard him gladly, but they could not accept His *"new* doctrine."

We cannot blame the Jews. We find the same mistaken zeal to-day, the same rejection of a higher truth not understood by our religious leaders. We remember it is recorded by Matthew, "All the *chief priests* and *elders* took counsel against Jesus to put him to death"; and again, "The chief priests and elders *persuaded* the *multitude* that they should destroy Jesus." Isaiah's words seem to be fulfilled: "The leaders of this people cause them to err."—*Isa. 9:16.*

Then, as now, the church of God refused to hear any doctrine new to it; it said: "We have Moses; we know that God spake unto Moses; as for this fellow, we know not whence he is."

Judge them not, Oh Minister of God, for "Wherein thou judgest another, thou condemneth thyself." It was no easier then to accept a "new doctrine" than it is now. It was just as hard to give up the old and sacred conceptions then as it is now.

"The common people heard him gladly." Those that were humblest in their opinions had little to lay aside, could come as a "little child" and receive.—*Matt. 11:25; 1 Cor. 1:19, 27.* But "The first shall be last." It is hard when we feel that we have so much of Truth, to humble ourselves to listen to "new doctrine"; to give up what has seemed so sacred, for a new idea.

Truth calls upon us to "Leave all and follow Me," even "Mother" and "Father"—our dearest past conceptions—for Truth's sake. "When that which is *perfect* is come, that which was in part shall be *done away.*"

The world has been crying for "more light," and then shrinks in alarm at the "new things," that "more light" reveals.

If we stand in a dark room, we see little that the room contains, we scarcely can tell where we are. If we stand in the kingdom of heaven, with our souls darkened, we cannot "see" what heaven is holding for us, nor know even *where we are!* Bring a light into the dark room, and how different everything appears; the light does not bring in anything, but it enables us to see what was already there, and to realize where we stand.

So the soul illumined sees everything in a new light, and begins to know where it is. This is the "new heaven and the new earth" promised—heaven and earth seen by a diviner light, revealing what was not seen by us before; *new to us.*

Jesus came as a light to the world, not to bring anything that was not always here, but to throw light upon the world. As it is written of him, "He came to bring life and immortality *to light.*" Men were suffering and dying not for any lack of good in the world, but because they did not know the truth, could not see the presence of Good.

He brought to light, or to man's consciousness, the immortality he had not known, and led man's thought out of darkness into light; out of ignorance into knowledge of truth; out of bondage into freedom.

"That is the light that lighteth *every man* that cometh into the world."—*Jno. 1:9.* But "If the light that is in thee be darkness, how great is that darkness." Every man has the light of the Divine within him, but if he becomes unconscious of this truth, he is in deep darkness to himself.

Jesus' mission was to show the Truth to man, and

thus rekindle the light of that Divine in man, by which he should see his way to the Father, and understand the tie that eternally unites him with his Divine Source. That "tie" is the Divine Nature in man, which Paul speaks of as the "Christ *in you*, your hope of glory." This unites man with God, and is the at-one-ment, which Jesus revealed, or brought to light. Only now is this being truly understood by man.

"The path of the just is as a *shining light*, which shineth more and more, until the perfect day." Our "light" within must increase until it blends with the Eternal, or enters the "Perfect day." At first, "We see through a glass darkly"—this is when understanding is feeble. "But then face to face." When our consciousness is clear, we see without any veil.

Truth is not changing—our light upon it is growing. Our forefathers lighted their rooms with a tallow candle. Electricity with all its possibilities was right with them, but they understood not its use. It was better to have a candle than no light, but would that satisfy them now? Would they not now accept the brighter light, and shall not we? Do we show disrespect to their memory when we use electricity instead of candles?

Do not let us put the new religious "light" out of our lives, because our fathers had it not. May we not imagine that they too have gone on into better light? We need not worry about leaving their light, they have left it too.

We pray for spiritual understanding, but are ready to refuse it, if it comes through a channel unknown to us. A simple story is told of a nest full of birds which were deserted by the mother-bird. Hunger beset them and an attempt was made to give them food for which they were crying, but as the strange hand approached them, their open mouths were quickly shut in a flutter of fear, making it impossible to give them that for which they cried. The food was then laid on the edge of the nest and they were left for the night. In the morning all were dead. Too afraid to take their food from a new source, and too blind to see it "at hand," they suffered and died for their own ignorance.

"May we not," says the writer, "for the same reason, lose the good sent to us in answer to our cries"?

The cry of these birds may be heard all around us. "Give us our spiritual bread, and our water of life, but give it to us in the old familiar way which we know so well."

One says: "It takes two to make a gift, one to give, the other to receive." God, the Giver of every good gift, has never withheld anything from us. David sings: "The earth is *full* of the goodness of the Lord."—*Psl. 33:5.*

If we lack *any* good, it is because we have not known how to accept and appropriate the good that is *every-where.* God has given *all; we* have not received.

"Our citizenship *is* in heaven."—*Phil. 3:20. Rev. Ver.* Not is going to be, but *is now.* The world needs a Saviour to-day just as much as it did 1,800 years ago. The same Divine Power, the same pure Life, the same Truth, the same Love, and the same spiritual Presence is with us. "Lo, I am with you always."

Let us *admit* this Presence and Power, and then shall we hear in each new voice that speaks the assuring words, "It is I, be not afraid."

If we follow the inner call of Truth, we shall have the outer evidence. The disciples, without a question, followed a voice *strange to them*, which bade them "come." They left all, and followed without any evidence. *After* this willingness and obedience, they received abundant proof; so will every disciple of Truth. Let us "Be careful to entertain strangers"—even strange, or new thoughts, "for thereby some have entertained angels unawares."   "With all thy getting, get understanding—for understanding is a wellspring of Life."— *Proverbs.*

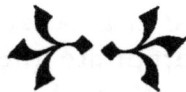

GOD.

OUR responsibility is twofold; first, to obey the truth as far as we understand it; and we read, "God gives his spirit to them that obey," which is to say, that more light comes to them that obey what light they have. The spirit of understanding comes in greater fulness to them that are obeying the Truth they already see.

But unless they are *looking for*, and ready to *listen to* higher understanding, they cannot receive the reward of their obedience! Hence, our second responsibility is to be ever on the alert for higher revelation, ever ready and willing to catch a hint of something beyond what we have yet thought of.

It is not a new Truth we seek but a new consciousness of Truth. What shall bring this new consciousness to us?

Jesus said to the disciples, " It is expedient for you that I go away; for if I go not away the Comforter will not come unto you." The "Comforter" is the Spirit of Truth, the *inner* guide. While Jesus is with the disciples, they look to Him personally. and leave upon *His* power and understanding. But His desire was to teach them how to be led by the spirit, which must be heard *within them*. Thus would their individuality be strengthened, and they learn, as each soul must sooner or later, to hear the guiding voice *within themselves*, and to come in *direct* touch with the Infinite.

This is true for every disciple. There is but one True Teacher. Jesus himself was learning from this One, and was showing to man, not what he personally could do, but what Divine Presence and Power, Divine Love and Truth, can do *in humanity*.

So he said to one who called him "Good Master," "Why callest thou *me* good, there is none good but one." As if to say, "I am not here to glorify myself, but God, the Father of All; if you see good in me trace it back of my personality, to the One Source of good which is Universal, therefore is for all alike. As I manifest this good, so may you. Greater works shall ye be able to do, but all by the One Power."

This inner guide, is that which shall lead us into new consciousness, it is called in Scripture, the "Still Small Voice," and of this leading it is written; "They shall be all taught of God."—*Jno. 6: 45.* This inner voice is the "Light that lighteth every man," which God has placed in each soul, to guide it into all Truth.

We cannot see by the light that lighteth another. We may get the spark that shall set our lamp to burning, from another's light, but that is all! It is written, "The spirit of man is the candle of the Lord," *Prov. 20: 27.* Whatever consciousness, or inner light any soul receives, it is set aflame by Infinite Love and Truth.

The voice of Truth keeps speaking in the soul, for it is always there, " Behold I *stand* at the door and knock." Once in a while some soul *hears*, and this is revelation! If it has ever been, it must be now, for Truth never changes.

The Whole Truth, includes all the fragments of Truth ever known. So that as we advance into better knowledge of Truth, we shall not lose any Truth we ever possessed. But one may ask, in what relation does a new Truth stand to the old?

We may find illustration for this in our schools, where

there are many grades, and a pupil passes from one to a higher, just as fast as he can accomplish the work required in each grade.

It is a pupil's pride to push on into new work, and learn new things; and it is a teacher's purpose to assist the child in his progression.

Each grade belongs to the one school, and has equal honor *in its place.* The last grade does not hold the first in contempt, but in high esteem, as having been a stepping stone in the way of advance.

One must learn his A B C's before he can become an author, and though he shape the world's thought by his writings, he never ceases to use his A B C's learned in the first grade.

No Truth gained is ever lost; the higher contains all the *Truth* of the lower.

Truth has been compared to a cone which has its base in a circle, and its summit in a point.

The circle well represents the eternal nature of Truth, and its omnipresence, encircling the universe.

But as the cone rises to its summit it terminates in a point, so as man's consciousness of Truth is lifted up, he begins to see the *unity* of all Truth. As it is written, "That in the fulness of times he might gather together in one all things in Christ."—*Eph. 1:10.* Christ is the final Truth into which all things shall be drawn. "If I be lifted up, I will draw all men unto me."

"Seek ye first the kingdom of God, and all these things shall be added unto you."

For centuries we have been pleading. "Thy kingdom come." If the kingdom is "at hand," and "within us," whence is it to "come"? It has already come. The Divine promise is, "Before they call I will answer," —*Isa 65; 24.*

Before we asked for the Kingdom to come, it was with us! *We* must come to a knowledge of *it*, and the result of our "seeking" has been to find it "at hand." And finding the kingdom, we find within it all good things,—ours, here and now.

Are we ready then, to hear a new doctrine, and to let the light within us be our guide? We desire better conditions, we long for satisfaction, but if we are unwilling to receive new ideas upon life, we shall have to continue to submit to old conditions, in the old ideas.

If the "*Spirit of Truth*," is leading us, we must expect to be led into more *spiritual* ideas of all things. Our conception of God, of Christ, of man and of life, will become more spiritual.

As our spiritual sense of things is quickened, we shall be glad to find our material sense being "done away." Jesus said, "The flesh profiteth nothing, it is the spirit that quickeneth," and we read that many of his disciples hearing this, "Went back, and walked no more with him," *Jno. 6: 60-66*; for they said, "This is a hard saying." They were not able to "bear" it, but shall not we search deeper into the words, and seek for their highest meaning?

May we not say with Paul: "Henceforth know we *no man* after the flesh; yea though we have known *Christ* after the flesh, yet henceforth know we *him so* no more?" *2d Cor. 5: 16*. For are we not going to search for the *spiritual* idea of God, of Christ, and of man?

Divine Science encourages this search, made by the light of Spirit. The name has a significance.

Science is "knowledge, Truth ascertained; knowledge duly arranged." Having for its foundation, or starting point, a Truth that never changes, all its knowledge is derived from, and agrees with this changeless Truth.

And this Science we are now to study, is Divine, because the Truth with which it begins and from which it judges of all things, is Divinity. God is the basis and foundation of all its knowledge.

For where shall we look for the changeless, but to God, the Eternal, "In whom is no variableness, nor shadow of turning." Where shall we seek for a beginning, and Source, Itself without beginning, but in the Infinite Mind of Wisdom and Spirit of Truth! Now this is our foundation, for in this Great Eternal Being, we shall find a Cause or Source, therefore a *reason*, for everything that is.

Let us then search in Spirit and in Truth for a clearer, and above all, a more *spiritual* understanding of this Great Being we call "God."

We read, "Other foundation can no man lay, than is laid, which is Jesus Christ." Here we learn that the foundation for Truth's building is already laid: like all Truth it is eternal!

"Order is heaven's first law," and the order in every building is, that the foundation shall be laid first. The strength and safety of the building depends upon the' perfection of its foundation.

What is the foundation of Divine Science?

The foundation for all Truth is "Jesus Christ;" not a personality, but the "Word" which was "In the begin‧ning with God, and was God." "All things were made by him," (Jno. 1:3) by the Eternal Word of God! With us always.

This Foundation and Cause of all things is in our midst today, and ever has been in the earth.

Of it Jesus said: "Before Abraham was, I am;" and again, "Lo! I am with you *always*."

How easy then to find and lay our foundation. It is God with us, and through us, above and below us— God everywhere present. "All in all."

Then, to know certainly the changeless Truth or real nature of all *things*, we must find the Truth of God.

First we will think of God as Source and Cause of all things; not making things of *nothing*, but of His own Life and Being, this Great Mother-Father God, brings forth all the forms of Life. "One God, and Father of all, who is *above all*, and *through all*, and *in you all*."—*Eph. 4:6.* "For *of* Him, and *through* Him and *to* Him are all things." —*Rom. 11:36.*

God the Source and the Cause, the Beginning and the end of everything; as Spirit saith: "I am the Beginning and the end"—"The first and the last." "I am *all* in the beginning, and *all* in the end. I am the *all* of *everything!*"

This is just what we mean by speaking of God as Principle, which is thus defined by Webster: "The source and origin; that from which anything proceeds; the beginning; the first,"

Principle is changeless Truth, Foundation and Cause, out of which visible things are brought forth.

God *is* the beginning of all things. Think of this! Everything that lives and moves, begins its life in God-Life. "With Thee is the fountain of Life." Everything true has its origin in God. All that is, is in and of God! We cannot emphasize this too much.

In the Word we read, "The same fountain cannot bring forth sweet and bitter water." From the same source cannot come sweet and bitter. Nothing can come from God, that is not *in* God. If the "fountain" or source of Life is sweet and good, it can send forth only that which is pleasant and good.

What then is the nature of this Fountain that supplies all Life?   What do we know of it?

We know that God *is good*, hence must say everything begins and ends in Good.   God never changes—if good, then always good, and sends forth only good to His creation.   "Oh, taste and see that the Lord is good." —*Psl. 34:8.* "For Thou, Lord, art good."—*86:5.* This teaches us then that the Source of life is good, and when I say with the Psalmist, (*87:7*) "*All* my springs are in Thee," I understand that everything that comes into my life has origin in this Great Fountain of Good.

Moreover, not only is God good, but all the good there is—as Jesus said: "There is none good but One." I cannot look anywhere else for my good, but to God.   I cannot find good in anything else.   I must look to God only for my good health.

I must know then where God is, and what God is, to know where and what my good is.

God is the Source of good.   God is the *only* source of good.   God is the source of *good* only, nothing else but good can come from God.

We know God not only as *a* Source and Cause, but as the *only* Source and Cause.   There is but *One Source.* "I am the Lord, and there is none else; there is none beside me."—*Isa. 45:5-6.* "One God and Father of all." "And Jesus answered, The first of all commandments is, Hear, O Israel, the Lord, our God, is One Lord."

We have thought it easy to believe in *One* God; but now that we find it means to believe in One Good; One Cause only, is it so easy?

We know God as Life; therefore as the only Life,

and the Only Source of Life; so it is written, "Whoso findeth me, findeth Life."—*Prov. 8:35.*

We know God as Love; as Paul says: "For God *is* love." Not Loving, but is love itself, and changes never! Love is God. "Every one that loveth is born of God." —*1 Jno. 4:7.* The source of everything is Love!

"God is Light."—*1 Jno. 1:5.* God is Truth. "I am the light of the world; I am the Truth," Jesus said. There is just One Light, One Understanding, One Intelligence, One Truth.

God is the Infinite Mind—All Wisdom.

"God is Spirit." God is Substance (*Sub*, under, and *stare*, to stand,)—"that which underlies all the outward." —*Webster.* Spirit is the one only Substance.

The *Substance* of all things is not the visible but the Invisible; is not matter, but Spirit. "The things that are not seen are eternal." We should rejoice in this. "Things are not what they seem," but altogether better ! So Jesus said: "Judge not by *appearances*, but judge righteous judgment."

Science teaches us to judge of things by their Source. If all things proceed from One Source, they are contained *in that* Source, before they are visible, and they can be only what that Source is.

We have seen that the Origin of all things is Light; is Love; is Good; is Spirit, or Intelligent Mind; is Truth, and, like a Great Fountain, this Light and Love, Truth and Life, is pouring forth its perfect Substance into all the forms of Life. In countless ways it is making itself visible to us.

But where shall we find this Great Source which is our Life, Substance and Intelligence? Do we say, like Job, "Oh, that I knew where I might find him, that I might come even to his seat"?—*Job 23:3.*   .

We long for God, because we long for Truth, for Peace, for Love, for Understanding, for Life. Jesus said that to know God aright is Life, eternal. Our desire for life, Peace and Good, is really our *cry for God*. Where shall we find Him? *Everywhere.* "In Him I live."—*Acts 17:28*. Think of this! I live in Life eternal, in Intelligence, in Spirit, in Truth and Love, in All Good. Of course I do if the kingdom of God is within me—at hand.

Do we believe that God is *Omnipresent?* We say yes; but think, do we believe God is *All*-Presence? "God omnipotent means good everywhere present," and this admits of no other presence but Good. Do we believe that God's Presence fills every spot and space, and do we refuse to see anything that is not the presence of Good? Yet this is just What *Omni*-presence means.

The Bible supports this idea: *Jer. 23:24*. "Do I not *fill* heaven and earth? saith the Lord." *Psl. 139:7*, "Whither shall I go from thy spirit, or whither shall I flee from thy presence? If I ascend into heaven Thou art there. If I make my bed in hell, behold Thou art there." God's presence, which, remember, means the presence of Changeless Love, Truth and Life, fills heaven and earth, and behold is to be found even in hell!

What is the difference between "heaven" and "hell"? Heaven is where God's presence is *recognized* as "all in all." Hell is where God's presence is not recognized. Both are "within" us.

But as if these words were not enough to convince us, we hear still further, in *Eph. 1:23*, about "The fulness of Him that *filleth all in all*"; and again, *Col. 3:11*, we read, "Christ is all and in all." This is what God omnipresent means.

Omnipotent—All-Power—admits no other Power.

God's Power is the Only Presence.   Can we accept this?
Paul says this very thing, in *Rom. 13:1*, "There is no power but of God."   Can we now admit an evil power or an
evil presence?   Can we claim any longer a Source for
evil?

Non-recognition of God as Omnipresence, Omnipotence, as All in All, is the only cause, presence or power
of evil.   Hence to recognize God as All-Presence, All-
Power, All-Intelligence, Omniscience, shall be the destruction of every *claim* of evil, error, or fear.

CONDENSED STATEMENTS.

"In the beginning was the word."
Divine Understanding begins with the word.
In imitation thereof we begin by speaking the word.
"The kingdom of God is within you."
"The kingdom of heaven is at hand."
God is Everywhere.   God is here.
God is Light.   Light is here.
God is Truth.   Truth is here.
God is Good.   Good is here.
God is Peace.   Peace is here.
God is Freedom.   Freedom is here.
Now am I in All Good Presence.
Now am I in Perfect Freedom.
Now am I in Changeless Love and Truth.
Now am I in Eternal Life.
Now am I in Full Light, for "I live, move and have my being" in God.   In Light, Truth, Love, Freedom, Goodness and Peace.
"God is All and in all."
"The *Truth* shall make you free."

"When ever the Christmas season
Lends lustre and peace to the year,
And the Ling-long-ling of the bells,
Tells only of joy and cheer,
I hear in the sweet wild music,
These words, and I hold them true:
The Christ who was born on Christmas morn,
Did only what you can do.

Each soul that hath breath and being
Is touched with heaven's own fire;
Each living man is part of the plan,
To lift the world up higher.
No matter how narrow your limits,
Go forth and make them broad,
You are, *every one*, the daughter or son,
Crown Prince, or Princess of God."

CHRIST, THE DIVINE MAN.

ALTHOUGH Truth may be Omnipotent, and perfect Love be Omnipresent; though we may "live move, and have our being" in God, the All-Good; though we dwell in the kingdom of heaven, if we are not conscious of these truths, and do not know the wonderfnl meaning to us, we may go our way, in lack of all things, losing the blessedness that is ours.

"Heirs of God, joint heirs with Christ," we may, through ignorance of this, be slaves of misery and poverty. As Paul declares: "Now the heir, so long as he is a child, (without understanding), differeth nothing from a servant, though he *be lord of all.*"—*Gal. 4:1.*

Truth must be recognized in order to be realized by us, and to become a power in and through our lives.

It is said that seed have been found in the hands of mummies, which being planted, have burst forth into growth, after having been dormant for centuries. The seed had within it all the Life-principle, waiting development, but *the hand that held it was dead.*

The Divine Life and Truth begins in the soul as a seed. It may be held in a dead consciousness, but the Truth-seed never dies. It is waiting its opportunity. It is implanted by Divine Hand in *every soul.*

One says, "When Jesus said he had finished the work, he had sown the entire field with seed; the seed were small, the harvest is *universal.*"

" We think that heaven will not shut forevermore,
Without a knocker left outside the door :
Lest some belated wanderer should come
Heart-broken, asking just to be at home,
So that the Father will at last forgive,
And looking on His face, that soul shall live.

We think there will be watchmen through the night,
Lest any far off turn them to the light.
That He who loved us into Life, must be
A Father, Infinitely Fatherly.
And groping for Him, all shall find their way
From outer darkness, through twilight, into perfect day."

"His mercy endureth forever."

"Every knee shall bow, every tongue confess."

What is this knowledge that we need to make us free?

The knowledge of God, and of man's relation to God; the right understanding of these will break the bonds of our captivity, and give us consciousness of Eternal Life.

Jesus said, knowing the Truth makes free, also knowing God is Eternal Life—two most precious boons, Freedom and Life, are ours for the knowing. Knowing what? That they *are* ours! "All things are yours," Paul affirms. Life and freedom are mine now. The Truth makes me *know* I am free. Understanding God and my relation to God, convinces me that I am Eternal Life, for I am *made* of Eternal Life. I am Peace, because I am made of everlasting Peace. I am changeless Love and Truth, for I am made of Love and Truth that changes never.

"I am, because God is." God is the reason or cause of my being at all; the Source and Substance of my existence.

All that I am must be found in God my Source, and

most truly I cannot be anything that God is not, for I have no other Source. God is all. I cannot be something else.

To know what I am, I must know what God is, for in God I have my beginning and in God I shall have my end. God is "All and in all."

What is God? Goethe says, "The *Most High* cannot be spoken in words." Then words, either written or spoken, can only hint of the highest conception of Truth, and each soul must go for itself to the Infinite Fount, to receive within its own consciousness.

To form a practical idea of God, take paper and pencil and write the word "God"; then write with this word every term that expresses God to you. Do not forget the Infinitude of God, and when you write beside the word God—"One"—write with it, "*All.*" The One God is all there is.

If you write "Mind," let the One Mind be *All* Mind; declare that the One Mind is all Mind; then cast out belief of something beside God, by *saying*, There is no other Mind, no mortal mind.

If you write the word "Love," let it be to you *All*. "Love fills all, I live in perfect Love. There is no fear or hate."

Whatever you write with God—"Life," "Strength," "Spirit," "Light," "Good"—declare it *All*. Deny the claim of any opposite. Make this a common practice if you would see God everywhere.

So we love to think of God as changeless Good, filling all: the Only Power, controlling all; Principle, or Source of Life, pressed out into all. Perfect Truth and Love, pervading all. Eternal Mind and Substance, sustaining all. Everpresent Fulness, supplying all. The

Only Intelligence enlightening all. "Since God is all, there is no room for any opposite."—*S, and H.*

Can any limited personality be attached to such an exalted idea of Infinite Being? Can we for a moment think that such an Universal idea of Deity, can be compatible with the cramped notion of God, as dwelling in any one time or place in greater fulness than in another?

"The fulness of Him that filleth all in all, without shadow of turning," must teach of Limitless Presence and Power, "That God may be all and in all," in every time and every place the same.

One says, "We are as much in the presence of God now, as we shall ever be." The only possibility is to become more and more conscious of God's presence. Our heaven is growing nearer, as our knowledge of God's presence expands.

To understand my relation to God, I must study Jesus Christ, for I am nothing to God except by and in the Christ.

"No man cometh to the Father but by me." Jesus Christ, we have been told, is the *foundation* of every created thing. All the universe of Spirit (and there is no other universe) is built upon Christ. What is the meaning of Christ? "Now know I no man after the flesh. Yea, though I have known Christ after the flesh, yet henceforth know I Him no more." If we will find the *spiritual idea* of Christ Jesus, we can then understand how every man is founded upon Christ, and how "Christ is all in all."

Many sayings of Jesus, which cannot refer to personality, will also be made clear to us, as "Before Abraham was, I am." "Lo, I am with you always." This "I am" that has been and shall always be in the world, cannot possibly be the personal Jesus, it must be something more. There is plainly reference to an impersonal presence. Also, when Jesus said of his disciples, "That they may be *one in us*, I in them and Thou in me," he must have referred to a spiritual or soul relation, and not to any personality.

"In the beginning was the Word, and the Word was with God, and the Word was God."—*Jno. 1:1.* Christ is here called the "Word" of God, which signifies the expression of God; or the expression of Life, Truth and Love. This eliminates all idea of personality.

A minister called the attention of his listeners to the fact that in the Gospels the name Christ applied to the Divine Nature of the Son of God, and the name Jesus to his human nature.

Let us try to understand Jesus' relation to God, for it is the type of every living soul. "I am the way," shows us that there is no other way. Jesus himself claimed no personal advantage over any one. He said, "I am the light of the world," also, "Ye are the light of the world." "As the Father hath sent me *even so* have I sent you." "The works that I do, shall ye do." "That the world may know that Thou has loved them as Thou hast loved me."

He showed what God could do in man, and that the Divine Power that governed him is universal, hence is for all alike.

One says, "Jesus solved the humam riddle; he has shown us in himself, that God and man are one inseparable life; God in Jesus, is God in our humanity."

Another declares, "Christ comes not merely to show Divinity to us, but to evolve the latent Divinity that is implanted in every one of us." Man was ignorant of the Divine in himself. The Truth, always there, lay dormant in his soul. Jesus was the first to rise out of this deadness of consciousness. He was the first of heaven's children, to know who and what he is—the Son of God. Paul speaks of this when he speaks of Jesus as "The *first-born* from the dead."—*Col. 1:18.* "The first-born of *every* creature."—*Col. 1:15.* Into his consciousness shall every soul follow, as fast as it awakens from its dream of ignorance.

By what Power did Jesus know and manifest the Divine Life and Truth? There is but One Power, One Presence, One Mind or Intelligence. Jesus recognized the One as All. He said, "Of *myself* I can do nothing." He claimed no individual power, no power but that which is universal, therefore is for all.

One says, "We must not try to imitate Jesus in his self-confidence." But was Jesus' reliance upon himself, or was it upon the One Divine Power and Presence, and shall we not imitate him in this?

Jesus' sole dependence was upon the Divine Nature which he was manifesting, the Christ or Expression of God, his own spiritual Being and Life. The same must be the strength and moving power of every living soul. Each one may say as truly as could Jesus: "I can do *all things* through Christ which strengtheneth me."—*Phil. 4:13.*

This Christ is the Whole Divine Nature, always with us, of which each soul is a partaker.

"Christ is all in all."—*Col. 3:11.* We need to accept this in its fullest sense, for then shall we come to see *Christ Only;* Begotten of God: Divine Self-hood; Divine Man, as all Self-hood, as the Only Man. Not seen "After the flesh," but in the understanding of God's Divine Idea of Man. All personalitiy is lost sight of.

This is the Foundation and Substance of every living soul. Christ is God's complete Idea for all men.

We are to come *into* Christ, by letting the old self "go"— die to our consciousness, and know Christ to be *all.* All therefore of me.

Jesus knew perfectly that he was nothing apart from the Divine, but recognizing his Divinity, declared all power, life, perfection and truth to be his, because of his relation to the Infinite. No other has yet comprehended this as Jesus did, but "All shall know Him."

"Beloved, now are we the sons of God, . . . but we know that when He shall appear, we shall be like Him." When we are *like Him,* he shall appear to us again. Then we shall be able to see Him.

"Christ *in you,* your hope of glory."—*Col. 1:27.* The Divine in you is your claim upon God, and through It and in It shall you be glorified.

> "In His Son the Father sees us,
> And as Sons He gives us place."

How shall I truly accept Christ as my *substitute?* By putting myself—as I have thought myself to be,—*entirely* out of mind, and where I have looked upon self, see Christ as the *Only* Self. I can then say with Paul, "*I no longer live,* but *Christ liveth* in me," or in place of the old me. This is true *self*-sacrifice, to be made "Once for all." We have been trying to patch up and make better the old self. We have repented of a sin here, and a short-coming there, and where the sin has rent the soul, we have tried to put in a new piece, a better condition. Shall we recall Jesus' words: "No man putteth a piece of new cloth into an old garment—for the rent is made worse."—*Matt. 9:16.* This is just what we have endeavored to do, to patch up our old lives with new Christ-life. What has been the result? Is sin destroyed and its effects banished?

If not, let us listen to the "new" way. Entirely *dis-*

card the old self; do not try to improve the mortal, but accept the Divine Self in its stead. If the Divine is exalted and the mortal denied a place, soon it will "No longer live," but the Divine will be all life.

"Likewise, *reckon ye* yourselves also to be *dead unto sin*, but *alive* unto *God* through Jesus Christ our Lord." This is to "Put on Christ."—*Rom. 13:14.*   Put out of thought the self that sins, and looking at Christ, or man's Divine Nature as *all* of man in God's image, declare: "Christ is *my* Divine Nature; Christ is my Life and Being; Christ is my Self-hood, when I find myself in God. I accept Christ as the All-Truth of me, for "Christ *is all and* in all."

Of such, the Divine saith: "Their sins and their iniquities will I *remember no more.*"   Having once truly accepted Christ, we can have no more memory of sin, but will say with Paul, "If I do that which I would not, it is *no more I* that do it." The Divine of me cannot sin, suffer, or be sick.

Continual sacrifice for sin is not Divine method, and is therefore not acceptable to Deity.—*Heb. 10:1-3, 5, 6, 8, 11-14.*

Accepting the Divine of us—Child of God—instead of the child of evil, we make a sacrifice "once for all," or rather accept the eternal sacrifice in Christ.

One says, "True humility is not to think meanly of oneself, but not to think of self at all." Accepting Christ instead of self is not to think of self at all; therefore not to think of the sinner. It is to be so filled with the Divine Idea of Perfection, Love, Goodness and Truth, as to have no room for any other idea.

Jesus taught the Divine Nature of man when he bade him say "Our Father." This declares man to have a Divine origin.   We say this is man's only nature, for there is no other origin.

Jesus emphasizes this when he bids us "Call no man on the earth your father, for One is your Father even God."   The command is, Acknowledge no Life-giver, no Source, or Cause but Spirit.

We have always recognized the "spark" of Divinity in man; why is it but a spark?   Is the Divine so feeble that it must yield the right of possession to another power?   No, for there *is* no other power !   It simply means that we have acknowledged the Divine so little that it has seemed but a spark to us.

Now, if we will exalt the Divine in man, lift it up, in all our ways acknowledge him, we shall soon realize the spiritual sense of Jesus' words: "If I be lifted up, I will draw all men unto me."   Truth will fan the "spark" into a great "flame" when we lift up Divinity in all.

CONDENSED STATEMENTS.

God is manifest to me through Christ within, "Because that which may be known of God, is *manifest in them.*"—*Rom. 1 : 19.*

I am heir of all good through the Divine in me. God only is my Father, Source, Origin, hence my only inheritance is good.

In the Divine of me, I am the child of God. I am the child of Good. Child of Light. I am born of Love. "I am free-born." I am child of Truth. I inherit all Good, all Love, all Light, or Knowledge, all Peace, all Wholeness.

I have no lack. I do not lack good. I have no lack of Love or Knowledge. I have no lack of Peace or Health, for "I" am Divine.

By the Christ, or the Truth, I am made free.

"If the Son shall make you free, then are ye free indeed."—*Jno. 8: 36.*

THE HOLY GHOST.

DIVINE CONSCIOUSNESS.

"THAT which is born of spirit is spirit." The child has the nature of the Father. If God is our "Father" we may rightfully claim to be of Divine Nature. Having been blind to this, all kinds of conceptions have gathered around ourselves—but "The Truth shall make you free."

We have heard of the artist, who looking upon a rough stone said, "There's an angel in that stone." There was no *visible* evidence of it, yet he began his work of chipping away, with patience and skill, bit after bit of the stone that hid the angel, until at last there stood before all eyes the visible representation. The artist mind saw the invisible angel, hidden beneath the rough exterior—so Divine Mind sees Divine nature buried out of sight perhaps in humanity, and with patience and skill destroys mortality's claims, one after another, until the perfect being is revealed.

What further endorsement do we find in the word of God, for the Divine in man?

In its first chapter we read: "God created man in *His own image;* in the image of God created He him;" and again in the same first chapter are these words; "And God saw *everything* that He had made, and behold it was *very good.*"

Is there anything that God did not make? *"All things* were made by Him; and without Him was not anything made that was made."—*Jno. 1: 3.* God made *everything,* and pronounces *all* He made "very good"; then there is no reality in evil.

Whatever there is, God is responsible for it, and more than that is the *Source* of it: there is "none else." "Whosover is born of God doth not commit sin, he cannot sin; *because* he is born of God."—*1 Jno. 1: 9.* "We know that we are of God." That which is born of God and cannot sin, is the Divine Man, the "Image and likeness" of God; for that which comes forth from God is like God.

As we have been admonished to call none other "Father," we must acknowledge ourselves born of God, and must know further that all that is born of God is pure and perfect. "Be ye therefore perfect even as your Father in heaven is perfect."—*Matt. 5: 48.*

"Be ye holy for I am holy."—*1 Pet. 1: 16.*

My only claim of perfection and holiness must be, because God my only source is Perfect and Holy. That which comes from God and is of God must be holy, the image of God cannot sin. Christ, Son of God, is the Divine Nature of all, and in the Christ, or *Truth* of myself, I am Divine. Jesus said, "I am the Vine, ye are the branches," and it is written in the same book: "If the root be holy, so are the branches."—*Rom. 11:16.*

Paul says, "That we may present every man perfect in Christ Jesus," which means spiritually, and in no other sense can any one be *in* Christ Jesus, that we may present every man perfect in the Divine of himself.

Man has never yet been bettered by condemnation; would it not be wise to try the opposite course? see the "angel" or the Divine Nature, the Christ presence in every soul, no matter how hidden; deny the truth of all seeming error; *it* is not born of God, and all that is *real is* of God.   Break away the false ideas that obscure the angle and watch the result.

"The worst way to improve the world is to condemn it.   Men might be better if we better desire of them." "Man is the image and glory of God."—*1 Cor. 11 : 7.* "Men, which are made after the similitude of God."— *James 3 : 9.*

It is certain that man in his spiritual nature is God-like, and when we see or understand but *One* Source, One Life, One Mind, and One Substance—Spirit—we shall know that man's true and only nature is Spiritual.   "God hath *made man* upright, but they have *sought out* many *inventions."—Ecc. 7: 29.*   Man has invented many false ideas about himself, and these false claims have gathered so densely about him, as to cover his "eyes" with a thick "cloud"; so that the inner glory of God is not recognized.

This "cloud" or veil, is "done away" when we see Christ, the Holy One of God as "All in all."   We "die" to the old idea of self which was false, and become alive to the Divine idea, the Eternal,—though "new" to us.

Paul beseeches us to put on this new idea of man · when he says:

"That ye *put off* concerning the *former conversation* the *old man"* (do not any longer talk about the man of sin; the man of God never sins), which is corrupt *according to the deceitful lusts*.   And be *renewed* in the *spirit* of your minds.   And that ye *put on* the *new man* (the new idea of man) which *after God,* is created in *righteousness* and *true holiness.—Eph. 4:22-24.*

The Bible gives full encouragement to look at God's perfect work, and to put away the old idea of unright-) usness.

If we once realize God as "All and in all"—*All that is in all*—we can never again admit the truth of something beside God. The source and cause of error and evil, is the belief in *something beside God.* A belief in two Minds, two Substances, two Powers, and two Truths, opposite to each other, is all the evil there is, and this belief is false.

"I am the Lord, and beside me there is none else." Let us get from this statement all the practical interpretation that we can.

The Lord is Life—All Life—then it may read: "I am All Life and beside Life there is none else, no opposite to Life." According to which we safely conclude there is no death. Life is All Power, All Presence.

What a joyful message if we can receive it!

The Lord is Good, All Good; then it may read: "I am All Good and beside Good there is none else." Which plainly states, there is no evil. Good is All Power and Presence.

The Lord is Spirit, then it may read: "I am spirit, and beside Spirit there is none else." This teaches us that all is Spirit, there is no other substance, no other Presence.

The Lord is Love, and so it may read: "I am Love, and beside Love there none else." There is no hate or fear. "Perfect love casteth out all fear."—*1 Jno. 4:18.* All is Love. The only Presence is Love.

If Spirit is *All*, then I am Spirit.

Spirit has no clouds and darkness. Spirit is Light; then I am Light.

Spirit has no sin, sickness, or death in it. Spirit is Holiness, Wholeness, and Life eternal. I am Holiness, Wholeness, and Life eternal. I am Understanding for I am Spirit.

"There is a Spirit in man and the inspiration of the Almighty giveth them understanding."—*Job 34:8.*

This "inspiration" of the Almighty is what we have known as the Holy Spirit, and here it is declared that this Spirit "giveth understanding."

The Holy Spirit of God is Divine Consciousness or Understanding, which illumines the soul, revealing to it the truth of the Infinite Love, Life, and Peace; by the Light of the Spirit each individual may know the unlimited Presence and Power of all Good, and may claim this Presence and Power as its own.

God is manifest to us visibly in Jesus.

"He that hath seen me hath seen the Father."—*Jno. 14:9.*

God is manifest to us in the Invisible in Christ, the Divine Nature in each.

"For that which may be known of God is manifest in them."—*Rom. 1:19.*

Christ is God's Divine Idea; in Christ we see what the Divine Idea is for *all.* The Light *by which* we see this Divine Idea, is Divine Consciousness, or the Holy Ghost. By this inner light are we led into all Truth, it is God-Consciousness within us.

The unpardonable sin is to refuse to see this Light, and to be led by it—for as long as we refuse its guidance we must remain in darkness, or lack of knowledge; by no other power can we be enlightened concerning our Source and our Divine Nature. The sin of ignoring the Light Divine must be given up, it can never be excused: by no other leading can we find the Father. This Holy Spirit guides us *from within*, it is the consciousness of God in the soul.

God is known as a Trinity in Unity called Father,

Son and Holy Ghost.   Our three lessons thus far have presented the spiritual idea of this Trinity.

God, the Infinite Mind of the Universe and man. Christ, the Divine Idea of the Infinite Mind.   Holy Spirit, the Divine Consciousness of the Infinite Mind. There is no perplexity in this understanding, to see how the Three are One.

Mind to be complete and perfect must have within it a Perfect Idea, and Perfect Consciousness.   Also, Idea and Consciousness cannot exist without Mind to contain and include them.

If we expect to accomplish anything, the very first fact is that we have an idea in mind of what we want to do, and how we want to do it.   All we do is based upon, and begins in that idea.   So Christ is the Idea in the Supreme Mind from which all created things begin.

That which enables a mind to carry out, or manifest its idea, is its consciousness—by understanding that it can do a thing our mind acts.   So the Holy Spirit is the *Acting* Power of Supreme Mind, by which the Perfect Idea it contains is carried into expression.

Christ is the Whole Truth of creation which is in the Infinite Mind *before* creation.   Christ is the *Universal* Man, the Divine Idea and Divine Nature of every individual.   This is what Jesus meant by saying, "I am the Vine"—there is just *One* Divine Man, "Only Begotten Son of God," "For whom the whole family in heaven and earth are named."   The "whole family" are the many "branches" of the one vine.   All individuals branch out from the One Divine Nature.

Study the parable of the vine and branches to under. stand how all individuals are related to the One Universal Man of God.

Christ is the "Vine," the root and beginning of all

living souls, which are the branches. Note the process when the vine begins to put forth its life in the spring; here and there are seen buds pushing their way out *from within* the *parent stem;* we know these buds are the first appearance of the great branches into which they shall grow; but all the life and substance of the branch still and always is drawn *from within* the vine. There is one vine, but many branches. Like to this is the relation of each and all individuals to the One Divine Soul. Divine Man is the Holy Root, there is but One Divine Man—individual souls are the many branches, pressed out from within the One Divine Soul, having life of its Life and substance of its Substance.

"If the root be holy so are the branches." When we see all in the Christ, and of the Christ, know the Christ or Divine Nature as the "root," we see also the purity and perfection of all.

But the vine with its branches which it has put forth, is not yet complete. A third necessity exists; from the branches must proceed fruit: if the branch adheres properly to the vine it bears much fruit, if it becomes severed from the vine, both branch and fruit wither and die. "Abide in me," says the "Vine," "and ye shall bring forth much fruit, for *apart from me ye can do* nothing."

The individual can be and do nothing of itself. Jesus represents the most perfect branch of this great Christ-Vine, and yet he said, "Of *myself* I can do nothing." He knew that apart from the great Principle of Life and Being, he individually could accomplish nothing. If *He* said it, we surely must.

The "Vine" is type of the Universal, Omnipotent, Divine Life, Substance and Intelligence, that is the only Source of individual life. It is Man, as Spirit. "*I am* Spirit." "I am the Vine."

The "branches" are type of individual life, substance and intelligence, *expression* of the Universal. "Man is the expression of God."—*Science and Health.* This is the living, active soul; Image of God.

The "fruit" is type of the visible universe; the earth; the spoken word; the true "body." The "fruit" is the inner Life and Substance, made visible; it is the third and last step in the Divine process. It has come from within Spirit; it is the "likeness" of God.

Hence the soul which is Man's individuality, is the Image of God, and the body is the likeness of God. There is but one life, and one substance for vine, branch and fruit; so there is but One Life and One Substance for Spirit, soul and body.

As the Vine, branch and fruit make one perfect and complete vine, so do spirit, soul and body make one perfect and complete Spirit.

Spirit is creator of the living soul, and soul is maker of the body, not of its own power, but by the Power back of the soul—even Divine Spirit.

One says, "Our natural bodies begin to form as soon our souls exist, and because they exist. The soul's life is the power that forms the body."

> "For of the soul, the body form doth take,
> For soul is form, and doth the body make."

"The mind of man is God,"—(*Science and Health*), for *All Mind* is God, there is but One Mind. Man, as Divine Being, is eternally in and of that Mind; as an individual, man *expresses* that Mind; thinks its thoughts, and then speaks these Divine thoughts into words, so the thought and word unfold *from within* Divine Mind; are contained within Divine Mind before they are thought or spoken.

We can learn from this the method or law by which

Infinite Mind expresses Itself, viz: Mind, forms its thoughts and speaks its words.

Let us compare these various statements:

1. Mind,	or Vine,	or Spirit,
2. Forms its Thoughts.	Forms its branches.	Forms its soul.
3. Speaks out its Word.	Puts forth its fruit.	Makes its body.

1st. Being.   2nd. Acting.   3rd. Result.

Back of you and me and all of us, is the Great Infinite One. As Jesus said, "My Father is the husbandman." Everything begins in this One known when manifest to us, as Christ—still One—for it is simply the Spiritual Truth and Life of the Father, expressed in all. "All are one in Christ."

The consciousness of Truth, Life and Love, or Divine Understanding is the Holy Spirit of God, the Light of the World, lighting each soul to see its Divine Nature, and to know that *all that is*, is Spirit, and its manifestation in soul and body; is Mind, and its expression in thought and word.

ONE. GOD. ALL.

One Mind is All Power.
One Life is All Presence.
One Substance is All Reality.
One Spirit is All Intelligence.
One Law is All Love.
One Good is All Truth.
All is Spirit.   All is God.
All is Mind.   All is Good.

If God is *Omni*presence, there is nothing *anywhere* but God.

There is no *presence* of evil.

If God is *Omni*potence, there is no opposition to God.

There is no *power* of evil.

If God is *Omni*science, there is no knowledge but of God.

There is no *knowledge* of evil.

There is no mind of evil.

There is no cause of evil.

"God is all and in all."

THE WORK OF THOUGHT.

THERE is no power against, or contrary to God. God is the Infinite or All Mind, of the universe. The whole Idea of creation is within this Infinite Mind, which also contains all consciousness.

Every idea in the world comes forth from the One Perfect Idea of God, for It is all. All Understanding in the world, comes forth from the One Perfect Consciousness, for It is all.

So God, as All Mind, Idea, and Consciousness, pervades all living souls, and acts within them. This action of Infinite Mind is called Divine Thought. Paul declares, "Not that we are sufficient of ourselves to think anything as of ourselves; but our sufficiency is of God."—*2 Cor. 3: 5.*

We are entirely dependent upon our Divinity for our ideas, our consciousness, and even our thoughts! When we receive the consciousness of this Divine Idea within us, Christ is born to us; and

> "Though Christ a thousand times in Bethlehem be born,
> If he's not born in thee, thy soul is all forlorn.
>
> Could but thy soul, oh man, become a silent night,
> God would be born in thee, and set all things aright."

I cannot claim to be anything in and of myself, or apart from the Infinite. What I am, individually, is wholly according to what the Great "I am" is.

The name "I am" is full of new meaning to us now. It

is not *originally* my individual name.   It is eternally the
the name of Divine Being.

The real "I" or self belongs in this Divine Being,
whose name is "I am."

There is but One I am. "I am that I am" is received
by Moses as the Divine Name.   It is becoming to us
a sacred name.   We have used the name "I am," as if it
belonged to us wholly, to handle as we chose; but now
we are learning to say "Hallowed be Thy Name."

We say "I am" in this understanding of it, with rev-
erence; for it is God's Name, it is God's Nature, it is
God's Presence, "descending upon *us* like a dove."

"I am" is always Life, Spirit, Love and Truth, filling
us to fulness, so that there is no lack, in that which I am.

"I am" is Wholeness, Perfection and Health, the
Mind of Good that is All in all.   There are not many I
ams, but One, even God.   So I understand that to say "I
am afraid, I am sick, I am weary, I am weak," is to
speak falsely; the *I am* is none of these things.

"I am," as I now speak it, is my "new name," because
it appeals to me with such new meaning.   "I will write
upon him my new name."—*Rev. 3: 12.*   I will give him
a new consciousness of my name.

Only my *Divine Nature can say I am.*   I have no being apart from God, "In Him I live, move, and have my
being."

To know *what I am,* I must know what the *All I am*
is.   Hence, when I say "I am," I speak not of myself but
of God.   It is enough to know what the Great I am is;
since It is *All,* It includes me.   To speak truthfully then,
I silence all opinions and beliefs, in order to *listen.* " Be
still, and know, (for then shall we know), that I am God."

Let us conceive of the individual as being perfectly
still.   In this silence of the soul, he hears the testimony

of the Spirit within him. "I am Spirit, . . . the beauty of holiness, the perfection of Being, imperishable glory, all are mine, for I am God. I give immortality to man, for I am Truth. I include and impart all bliss, for I am Love. I give Life without beginning and without end, for I am Life. I am Supreme and give all, for I am Mind. I am the Substance of all because I *am that* I am."—*Science and Health, page 149.*

When the individual soul thus hears from within, it has "become a silent night," and Truth is forming *itself* in soul and body. Our thoughts are being put out, that the Divine may do its own thinking in us, and speak its own words.

"For it is not ye that speak, but the Spirit of your Father which speaketh in you."

Many mistake the intention of these high declarations, supposing the individual is speaking of himself, but instead of this he has put self *out of the way*, and is letting the spirit of God speak through him.

This spirit spoke through Jesus, (as he said, "The words which I speak, I speak not of myself") What did it say?

"I am the light of the world." "I am with you always." "I am the Truth. I am the Life." "I am the resurrection and the life." "I and my Father are one." "Abide in me." "He that liveth and believeth in me shall never die." "Come unto me." "In me ye shall have peace," etc.

This "I am" and "me" is the Divine Nature of which we have been speaking, it says the same words within each, for Jesus spoke not these words of himself individually, but of the Father, or Spirit of Truth.

When we learn to speak the I am rightly, we have

found a refuge from every ill! Into it we may run and escape every claim or belief of mortality.

When we go into the "I am" we enter God's World. Spirit's realm.

It is in *our own* little world, which means our belief of separation from God, that sin and evil exist.

There is no sin in God's World; no evil in God's universe, no darkness in God's presence, and God's world is the only world. God's universe fills all, God's presence is all in all! Hence a world of sin, evil and darkness, is a false belief. There is no world of our own, apart from God.

My belief in a world of sin, is my mistake, resulting from my idea of separation.

Jesus came into *our* world, came to us in our *belief* of separation from God, to show us the truth of our oneness with God.

"I have overcome the world"; not God's world, but the false idea of the world, the world and the self apart from God that we have believed in. The truth shall make you free.

The world of separation has no true existence, for God is all in all. It is therefore a belief which Truth destroys; in this belief of separation is all the claim of sin and suffering.

To destroy or overcome this world of suffering, man must come into consciousness of oneness with God; this ends our belief of separation, and is the end of *our* world of sin and death.

Then we see the "new earth," or God's World filled with Divine Nature.

Oneness with God is the at-one-ment.

In this concious oneness, self is surrendered. God is all; then we say, I am what God is, for I cannot be something beside God. Therefore I let God, or "The Spirit of My Father," say within, "I am Life Eternal and Changeless. I am Spirit and Power. I am Light and Truth. I am Fulness and Freedom. I am Health, Goodness, Perfection, and all Love."

This is what I am, for there is no other "I am." I think this that I am, and my soul is radiant with Light. Then I speak what I think, and my body is full of Light, full of Strength, full of Good, full of Health, because I see what I am.

There is no "I am," no Being anywhere, that is not *in* Peace and Health.

In thus thinking, "We have the mind of Christ."—*1 Cor. 2: 16.* And are willing to "Let the word of Christ dwell in us richly in all wisdom."—*Col. 3: 16, 17.*

"And whatever ye do in word or deed do all in the *name* of the Lord Jesus, giving thanks to God and the Father by him."

The "name of the Lord Jesus" is this very "I am" that we are to believe in and to abide in, for it is the Great Christ presence which includes all, "I in them and they in me." "That they may be *one* in us."

As soon as I see the One that I am, I can also see what I am not!

I begin to think of the true I am; I know that I live in Mind and not in body.

I am spirit, and am manifest in soul and body.

I am Mind, and am expressed in thought and word.

We have studied Mind, and have found the meaning of Its threefold aspect. We have seen the Son to be in the Father. This is the place *Divine Man* holds, he is co-eternal with God, therefore *is* Eternal Life, Changeless Truth, and Perfect Substance. The many living souls are but branches out of the One Man and therein have they all Life, Being, Intelligence, and Substance. The fruit of these branches is the body, perfect and complete in all good when the branch abides in the vine.

Thought is the busy worker; gathering material from within, from Source and Cause Invisible, from the I am that is always Wholeness and Perfection, it conveys what it has gathered into the visible, or fruit.

Thought is building the visible universe, and if it turns only to spirit for its knowledge, the outer will be in the very likeness of Spirit.

If we see in our visible "world" things contrary to good or God, then thought has turned away from Spirit to gather its material for building, and brings forth other than Spirit's fruit, "For the fruit of the spirit is in all goodness and righteousness and truth."—*Eph. 5:9.*

Misery, error, and evil, are not fruits of Spirit. Has thought power to bring forth these?

It is written, *Jer. 6:19,* "Behold I will bring evil upon this people, even the *fruit of their* thoughts," and again "As a man thinketh in his heart so is he."

The soul of man is the power God has given him to think divinely, and thus image all Good. If thought has been wedded to something beside Spirit, it has failed to image God in the earth. Among the wonders shown to Christian in the Interpreter's home, was a man raking in the dust, and so intently was his attention fixed upon this, that he did not see held just above him a crown, waiting for the upward look of his eye, and the lifting of his head.

"Thou hast crowned him (man) with honor and glory. Thou hast put *all things* under his feet," but, thought has been so busy looking into the "dust" of its own stirring up, so intent upon seeing man as a "worm of the dust," that it has not seen the crowning of man by

Divinity, nor lifted its head to receive the God given glory!

Now by Divine Consciousness, are we able to see man by a Diviner light. We are beginning to believe in the Divine Idea of Man and to accept it as all of man.

When thought sees truly what is in Being or Source, all things will *appear* right and good, for "Thoughts expand into expression."—*S. and H.*

Body is the thought made visible.

We must therefore carefully guard our thinking. Let Truth and Divine Consciousness, which speaks only of good, control it.

"Stand, porter, at the door of thought."—*S. and H.* Guard the very entrance of thought, decide whether God's Idea alone shall enter your thought. You can decide, for you are the thinker.

"If we are wise," says one, "We will not permit anything to enter our thoughts, that we are not willing to have expressed in our bodies." "Think the thoughts of Infinite Mind. Watch your thinking, control it with Truth. There is a channel, so to speak, through which the Light (of Divinity, the Life, the Perfection, Wholeness, etc.) is conveyed to its destination, and this channel is man's capacity to think."

Perfect Life, Divine Peace, all Goodness and Health, Intelligence and Freedom, are all ours, for "We are Christ's and Christ is God's"—*1 Cor. 3:23.* Thought is the "channel" by which these Divine qualities are conveyed to their destination. Their *destination* is *the body*. Thought should continually pour into word and body, all perfect qualities contained in Divine Source. Thought and conditions of body are as Cause to effect; change the thought, and conditions of the body will change.

I must be the Mind of Good, before I can think good, or act good.

Good thinking comes from Good Being, and good doing results from good thinking.

I cannot make myself good by *acting* good! I must begin where all things begin, in Being. See the truth of my Being. I am Good, is first; I think good, follows; I act and speak good, is the result.

I am perfect in Mind, for Mind is God.

I am perfect in Thought.

I am perfect in body.

SILENCE SELF, AND LISTEN.

"Be still, and know that I am God."

I am

Mind, Idea, Consciousness.

"In him dwelleth the fulness of the God head bodily; and of *his fulness*, have all *we* received, and grace for grace."—*Col. 2:9; Jno. 1:16.*

I am the fulness of the God head bodily.

In Source I am Life, Strength, Intelligence, Love, Wholeness, Freedom, Fulness, Goodness, and Truth.

In Source I have power to *express* Life, Strength, Wholeness, Goodness, Etc.

In Source I am *conscious* of having power to express my Wholeness, Strength, Life, Etc.

I know the Truth of Being Whole.

"In him ye are complete."

I think of my freedom and peace.

I declare now my strength and completeness.

By the Law Divine, as I recognize and declare my Peace, Plenty, and Satisfaction, the Truth of Peace, Plenty and Satisfaction resounds through all my existence.

The One Only Voice that speaks "I am Peace," is God. My soul and body echo that voice and say "I am Peace."

THE TRUE I AM.

Lite.
Love.
Peace.
Strength.
Health.
Goodness.
Perfection, etc.

I think what I am.
I speak what *I think* I am.
Result of thought :   The body full of Life, strength,
health, etc.

THE FALSE I AM.

Life *and* death.
Love and fear.
Peace and discord.
Strength and Weakness.
Health and sickness.
Goodness and evil.
Perfection and imperfection.

I think what I am.
I speak what *I think* I am.
Body the *result* of what *I think I am.*

Which "I am" have we been thinking, the true or
the false? The body answers our question; well and
sick; strong and weak; living and dying.

OUR JUDGMENT DAY.

EVERYTHING begins in mind, is expressed in thought, and manifest, or spoken forth in word.

Mind is the Actor, or Thinker. Thought is the action, and word is the fruit or result. Every action must have an actor before it, and a result following it.

Every thought must have a thinker preceding it, and a spoken word following it.

Mind is the *spirit* of Man; his Divine Being and Life, his Intelligence and Substance.

Thought is the *soul* of Man. Image of Eternal Mind, Life, Being, Intelligence, and Substance.

Word is the *body* of Man, that which results from thought, which shows forth thought, likeness of Eternal Mind, Life, and Substance.

Thought is the *invisible form* of Mind, Life, etc.

Body is the *visible form* of Mind, Life, etc. "By one spirit are we all baptized into one body."

When all have One Mind, One Intelligence, and that the Mind of Christ or Truth, we shall see but one kind of body, perfect and pure.

When we see no Cause but Infinite Mind, we shall see no result but a perfect body.

Mind works through thought into word. Spirit works through soul into body.

Mind is the Only Power, and Cause of everything. All things begin to form in Mind.

Thought is the action that forms things. The work

of the soul is to form the Image of the Divine within it-self, and to bring Its likeness into the visible.

Body is the thing formed by this action. The body of this perfect method is the likeness of God—the fruit of Spirit.

Stillness is the Universal Man, the "I am"; enter therefore into the silence, if thou, my soul, wouldst learn what I am.

Action is the individual man, expression of God, manifestation of Divinity.

Mind is the Universal Man, Fulness and Freedom.

Thinking is the individual man; the Divine Acting, declaring itself.

Spirit is the Universal Man, Changeless Self-hood.

Living soul is individual man, "Thought of God," as Phillips Brooks has said; Image of God, action of God.

Thought stands between the Invisible and visible. By the action of thought is the Invisible made visible; this is the law of expression.

Divine Thoughts are the angels of God; Love Messages straight from the heart of the Infinite Soul, to the living soul—the spiritual "ear" of man. "Angels are pure thoughts winged with Truth and Love. Angels are not messengers, but messages of the true idea of Divinity flowing into humanity. These upward soaring thoughts, never lead mortals to self, or sin, but guide them to the principle of all-good."—*Science and Health*.

"When the angels look into the soul of man, they see only the good and true."

> "And it seems to me that the more we grow,
>   Like the angels in love and duty,
> The less we shall see of evil in all,
>   And the more of good and beauty.
> And so the good shall increase, increase,
>   And evil shall vanish away,

. Until the Truth in each heart shall glow,
Like the light of a perfect day."

When "The Lord is in the midst of thee," (in the midst of thy thoughts), "Thine eye shall not see evil any more."—*Zeph. 3: 15.*

In our ignorance of God, and belief of separation, we have conceived of two selves, a spiritual nature, and a carnal nature. The latter is the sinner, the former the saint. One the child of the evil one; the other child of God.

Both of these natures, our belief declares, inhabit our tenament of clay, though they are opposed one to the other. Conceive of deadly enemies living together in one house! Would we expect very much peace or harmony in that house? Yet under just such circumstances, as we have supposed, we have been trying to find health and peace of mind!

One speaks to us of peace; the other holds us in bondage. "Nevertheless what saith the scriptures? *Cast out* the bond woman and her son; for the son of bond woman shall not inherit with the son of the free woman." —*Gal. 4:30.*

We are to cast out of our mental household the thought, or belief of bondage to "the world, the flesh, and the devil," and the fruit of such thought will also go, for "We are not children of the bond woman but the free. *Stand fast* therefore in the liberty wherewith Christ (the Truth) hath made us free, and be not entangled again with the yoke of bondage."—*Gal. 5:1.*

We "*put off* the old man," the self apart from God, the "sinner" that must die, when we see Christ,—Divinity, "I am," as *all*. It is simply growing out of self into Christ, after we receive the revelation that came to Paul, of which he said, "It pleased God to *reveal* His Son *in me*."—*Gal. 11:5.*

When self is dead, Christ is all.   The growth out of self is strongly pictured in these words:

First, "All of self and none of Thee.

Second, Some of self and some of Thee.

Third, Less of self and more of Thee.

Fourth, *None* of self and *all* of Thee."

"There is therefore now no condemnation to them that are *in* Christ Jesus.   For the law of the spirit of life, in Christ Jesus, (perfect idea of man), *hath made me free* from the law of sin and death."—*Rom. 8:1-2.*

"If ye be led of the Spirit, ye are not under the law." —*Gal. 5:18.*

"Reckon ye yourselves therefore, to be *dead unto sin,* but alive unto God."—*Rom. 6:11.*

We have not seen the impossibility of accepting Christ, and still holding on to the sinner!   But we must receive Christ as *all.*   See no more condemnation, no law of sin, no bondage to the ills of the flesh, no self but Divine Nature, the all that I am.   This means perfect freedom to us, and wholeness in spirit, soul and body.

"In the spiritual philosophy of Jesus, religion and health are viewed as one.   Health of body was external holiness, and holiness was internal health."

"How shall we take hold of this new realization? By using the new thoughts and speaking the new words faithfully.

See what I am, think and declare it.   See what I am not, cast it away by denying it."   "Know ye not, that to whom ye *yield yourselves* servants to obey, his servants are ye, whether of sin unto death, or of obedience unto righteousness."—*Rom. 6:16.*

"Be ye transformed by the *renewing* of your minds."

"Finally, whatsoever things are pure, are true, are lovely, are of good report—*think* on these things."—*Phil. 4:8.*

The more steadfastly we think upon good, the less of evil shall we see; the more earnestly we think upon Peace, the less of discord shall we see, the more we think upon righteousness, the less of sin shall we see; the more we think upon Health, the less of sickness shall we see.

Not that thought has this power in and of itself, but good thought, health thought, life thought, *expresses God*, and fulfills the law of all Being, of all Mind, therefore the law is *completed* in good results of health, peace, and rightness. It is the law of God.

If we will listen to the general conversation around us, what shall we hear? Constant acknowledgement of God, the Good? Do we talk of good health, and perfect love, or is our talk of ill-health, and much fear? Our speech shows what our thoughts are. If thoughts mold our conditions, is it any wonder that in every direction there are signs of sin, sickness and death? The outer is but an expression of the inner.

The light of Truth shining more clearly within us, shows us our mistakes, uncovers error and destroys it for us.

In this light we now discover many opinions and beliefs, not based upon changeless Love. We believe so many things that could not come from changeless Love, which are to be separated from our thought and cast out. We cannot talk as we once did, for we do not think the same. "From the abundance of the heart the mouth speaketh."

We are trying to "Let love become a habit of the soul," as Drummond says: to let good become a *habit* of thought. In order to do this, we are led to deny a place to evil in our thoughts, somewhat as Paul says, *Eph. 4:27,*

"Neither *give place* to the devil." When we see God everywhere, we cannot consent to allow evil a place. There is no place for it. When we see Truth clearly, we cannot give error a place. When we recognize Love as Infinite, we can find no place for fear. If Life is all, death has no place. Seing Perfection fill all, we can grant no place to imperfection.

Truth revealed, shows us the One All, without any opposite, and says to claims of evil: "Depart from me, I never knew you"; which is to say, you are not of Truth.

Jesus said of the devil, the personification of all error, "He was a murderer from the beginning, and abode not in the truth, for there *is no truth* in him." "For he is a *liar*, and the Father of it." The origin of all evil is a lie. It says, There are two minds, two wills, two powers, etc., and all sorrow and trouble come from this falsehood.

Now we are beginning to separate and to cast away from the self all that the I am is not, and to maintain firmly that which I am.

This process into which I find myself drawn, *began* in the first dawn of spiritual consciousnees. When man awakened from the "dust," or from the wholly material conception of himself, and "Became a living soul," (*Gen. 2:7*), he became alive to, or conscious of the fact of his spiritual being. He heard Truth saying *then*, even though he heard in feeble consciousness, "Thou shalt not partake of the knowledge of good and evil."—*Gen. 2:17*. This is the interpretation we may find beneath the letter of those words.

Later on, man receives the same instruction under another figure. "Thou shalt not sow thy field with mingled seed."—*Lev. 19:19*. "For what a man soweth that shall he also reap." Another way of saying, Thou shalt not believe in good and evil, for if thou dost, thou shalt reap good and evil.

Jesus represented this condition of thought by a parable (*Matt. 13:24-30*). He illustrated the good seed by "wheat," and the evil seed by "tares." He saw thought as a field sown with mingled seed. The kingdom of heaven, which is "within you," was planted with good seed only; but *men fell asleep*, and *in their sleep* saw "an enemy" planting tares! *Asleep* to Truth, we see an opposite to Truth. This is the "origin" of evil.

So good and evil are held side by side, (*26*) until thought awakens to the fact of good as all; then it questions, "Whence the tares"? It did not know before, that the tares had *no right* to be there. Something is arousing thought, and it at once desires to separate the wheat from the tares.

This shall be done, Truth replies, "In the time of harvest." Then "I will say to the reapers: Gather ye together first the tares and bind them in bundles to burn them, but gather the wheat into my barn."

Our first question has been, since Light revealed the true nature of all things as good, "Whence then is evil"? Truth answers: *You have been asleep!* The harvest is the awakening time of thought. It is called in other places, the Judgment day.

To judge is to discern, or distinguish between; and our "Day of Judgment" is when by Divine Light within, our thoughts are able to distinguish, and thus separate, between the true and the false claim.

The "Reapers" are Divine Thoughts, directed by Truth, in this sifting and separating. We understand the process when we have entered into it.

What is Truth's directions? "Gather *first* the tares

and bind them to burn them." Error must be disposed
ol first. This law we will consider in our next study.

"Gather the wheat into my barn." All good is eternal. All error shall be consumed. "For behold the day
cometh that shall burn as an oven."—*Mal. 4:1.* The
"Day" is the Divine Light; it shall "burn as an oven,"
for "Our God is a consuming fire," consuming all unlike
good. The Light is also the fire, for the Light of Truth
destroys all error belief.

Jesus again illustrates this judgment, in *Matt. 25:31.*
Truth is the Judge; sitting upon his "throne," represents
the Truth enthroned within our consciousness. Then is
judgment passed upon all conditions, and separation is
made by Divine Thoughts, for the "holy angels" are in
this picture. The "sheep" are placed upon the right,
the "goats" upon the left. The sheep go into life eter-·
nal, the goats into the everlasting fire.

These all teach us of the purifying each soul receives, when it falls into the hands of Truth. Every belief of sin, error, evil, or any opposite to God, shall be
dissolved in the consciousness that the One is All.

"I will turn my hand upon thee, and purely purge
away thy dross."—*Isa. 1:28.*

PRACTICAL SUGGESTIONS.

When we look into faces around us, we find traces of anxiety and care in all. Anxious thought has written its marks over most faces.

What are we anxious about? Some fear haunts us. We seem afraid of so many things. Afraid of *falling* into something that will hurt us, or somebody else. Suppose now, that we just *let ourselves fall!* Rest awhile by saying, "I have no concern about what happens. I am not anxious. I have no responsibility." It will be well for us to try falling for a time. We have been on such a strain, trying to *hold ourselves up,* to keep from falling; let us now yield, give up the strain, fall! What then? Where is there to fall but into God?

"Underneath are the everlasting arms." We have never rested upon them, because we have been trying to keep *ourselves* up. When we "let go," we shall feel all about us, these strong arms."

All threats of what may happen to us, will be *proven* powerless when we give up resistance. Let come what will, for only God can come!

We may begin to destroy claims of fear and anxiety by saying often: "I. am not afraid, for there is nothing to be afraid of. "God hath not given me a spirit of fear. Perfect Love casts out all fear."

I am love, for God is Love. I am peace, for God is Peace. I am understanding, for God is Understanding. I am not afraid,

In the judgment of Truth, we are led to surrender past conceptions, that we may follow the light of a new consciousness. "And another of his disciples said, 'Lord, suffer me first to go and bury my father.' But Jesus said 'Follow me; let *the dead* bury their dead.' So, likewise, whosoever he be of you that forsaketh not all that he hath, he cannot be my disciple.

"If any man come to me, and hate not his father and mother, and wife, and children, and brethren, and sisters, yea, and his own life also, he cannot be my disciple.

"The kingdom of heaven is like unto treasure hid in a field, the which when a man hath found, he selleth all that he hath, and buyeth the field."—*Jesus' words*.

Martha was cumbered about much serving; and Jesus said to her, "Thou art careful and troubled about many things. But one thing is needful; and Mary hath chosen that good part which shall not be taken away from her."

We cannot receive the Divine Idea of All-good, until we have given up many opinions and beliefs,

FASTING.

"WE shall all stand before the judgment seat of Christ."—*Rom. 14: 10.* That which cannot "stand" or remain, before Truth's judgment, is not of Truth.

"We shall all stand" before this judgment, is a blessed assurance, that there is Truth enough in all, to abide the trial by Truth! And Paul adds right here, (*Rom. 14:11*) as if this is what was in his thought, "For it is written, As I live, saith the Lord, *every* knee shall bow to me, and *every* tongue shall confess to God."

"Judgment day" comes, when the Light of Divinity is so bright in the soul, that it detects all that is of Truth and all that is not of Truth—all that is of the Divine, and all that is not.

In this time, or consciousness, sinners "tremble" because all sense of error is about to be destroyed; only that which is of Divine image and likeness, shall "remain," or "stand," in this increase of Light.

So it is written, *Psl. 1:5.* "The ungodly, shall not *stand* in the judgment," but *"We* shall *all* stand!" All that is ungodly anywhere, shall be wiped out! Truth shall search out all wickedness until none is found.—*Psl. 10:15.* "The wicked shall be turned into hell,"—*Psl. 9:17,* that is, into the purifying fire which is Divine Love.

"For yet a little while and the wicked *shall not be.* Yea, thou shalt diligently consider *his place,* and *it shall not be.*"—*Psl. 37:10.* Because in the very place that we saw wickedness, Light and Truth have shown God to be! Omnipresent Good. In this light the wicked shall not stand or remain in any place at all. Omnipresence is the "Consuming fire."

"As wax melteth before the fire, so let the wicked *perish,* at the presence of God."—*Psl. 68:2.*

"When the Lord shall have washed away the *dross* of the daughters of Zion, and shall have purged the blood of Jerusalem from the midst thereof, by the spirit of judgment, and by the spirit of burning."—*Isa. 4:4.*

"The sinners in Zion are afraid. Who among us shall *dwell* ("stand") with the devouring fire? Who among us shall *dwell* with the everlasting burnings? He that walketh uprightly, and speaketh righteously, he that stoppeth his ears from *hearing* of blood, and shutteth his eyes from seeing evil."—*Isa 33:14-15.*

When the time of judgment or separation comes, the sinners are represented as being "afraid," or "trembling," or being in great rage, because their end is near. As in *Rev. 12:12.* "The devil is come down unto you, having great wrath, because he knoweth that *he hath* but a *short time.*" Later on in the book, we see the devil cast into the "Lake of fire." The Greatness of Divine Love, at last consumes the most boasted power of evil.

The purifying fire, then, is a process in each soul by which all false conceptions, are destroyed. Paul tells all about it in *1 Cor. 3:11-16,* (please read it right here). Upon one foundation, which is Truth, men are building two ideas of life; one is of Divine Nature, therefore is the eternal Substance, designated as "Gold, silver, and precious stones." The other is not of the Divine Nature, Changeless; Truth, and it is designated as "Hay, wood, and stubble," because of its perishable nature.—(*12*).

The testing time comes.—(*13*). "The day shall declare it." Divine Light shall show the true or false nature of all things, of all opinions and all works. "The fire shall try every man's work of what sort it is."

If man's idea of life is based upon the true and eternal, his thought and word, his soul and body, is representative of Truth, is the image and likeness of God. This building "abides," "dwells," "stands" in the midst of Light and fire.—(*14*).

If man's ideas of life are contrary to that which is good, his thought and word, soul and body, is representative of error. This *building* "shall be burned" in the consuming fire. All the false ideas of life shall be destroyed; all that this soul has "built" shall be swept away, in order that his thought may be purified, for it is declared, (*15*),

"But *he himself* shall be saved, yet as by fire."

This judgment day, by the "light" of which we are able to discern what is of Truth's nature and what is not, and therefore to separate the true from the false claim, does not break suddenly upon us, but comes at the end of a process within our consciousness.

It is the "Day of the Lord," which spiritually interpreted signifies the "Light of the Divine Nature," the light in which Divine Nature is clearly seen.

It is a day of destruction, which we welcome when we understand it, because the many false ideas which our ignorance has invented, are destroyed by the true light.

This judgment day comes near the "End of the World," because in its light, our conception of the world passes away and we enter into a new consciousness of the world. Thought is ready to see heaven and earth by a

new light, is prepared to receive a new idea of heaven
and earth; this is the end of *our* world!

John saw in his vision, the "Great and small" appear before God to be judged.   In this judgment he
saw heaven and earth pass away; he also saw "Death and
hell cast into the lake of fire."   Later, he declares that
he saw a "New heaven and a new earth," but speaks not
of seeing a "new hell" after its destruction!

The devil spoke to Jesus, "All these things will I
give thee if thou wilt *worship me*." Worship acknowledges
a power and presence.   Every day this temptation meets
us, as it did Jesus; evil appearances appeal to us, to acknowledge the reality of evil, to admit its power and
presence!   But Jesus answered, "It is written, Thou shalt
worship the Lord thy God, and *Him only* shalt thou
serve."   Truth replies to claims of error, God alone is
power and presence; this only do I acknowledge.

Then "the devil leaveth him and angels come.'

We recall the story of the Saint, who was so lost in
contemplation of Divine Love, as to be filled completely
with its Holy Presence.   In the midst of his bright vision
arose a dark figure, whom he knew to be "Satan." Looking upon it a moment, with the light of Love filling his
soul, he exclaimed, "Satan, thee too I love."   Immediately the dark form disappeared, and Light Divine, shone
in the very place where darkness had been.

To look at every appearance, with thought aglow in
the consciousness of Divine Presence and Power as *all*, is
to dispel every opposite claim.

Peter expresses this idea of the judgment day when
he says, "The day of the Lord shall come as a thief in the
night."

A thief does not *annouuce* his coming with noise of

trumpet and commotion! He steals upon us so silently, that we are not aware of his presence, until we see what *his work* has been!

So does Divine Light quietly take possession of our thoughts, stealing away our treasures of earth. As is added, "In which the heavens shall pass away with a great noise, and the elements (of the world) shall melt with fervent heat, and the works that are therein shall be burned up."

The Light is the thief; we now long for its coming! though we shall find all our old and highly valued ideas of heaven and earth "done away."

Understanding the work of Light, even its destroying power, we no longer rebel, but gladly lay in its consuming power, all that is not of Divine Nature.

"He shall baptize you with the *Holy Ghost* and with *fire*." Christ's baptism upon us, immerses us in Divine Consciousness, which purifies us from our beliefs in something beside God.

We noted how Truth said in this harvest, or sifting time, "Gather first the tares, to burn them."

First then, we will search truly among our conceptions, and separate, by the light of judgment, based upon Spirit as All Life, Mind, and Substance, all that *claims* to be, or that we have believed to be a truth, a life, and a mind not God.

We can do this when touched by Divine Knowledge, for "He that is spiritual judgeth all things."

Standing in the Presence of Truth, let us witness what separation is made between the Divine, and not Divine.

On one hand we have:	On the other:
The Divine Nature.	The claim of mortal nature.
Born of God.	Not born of God.
Cannot sin.	Full of sin.
Perfect health.	Full of sickness.
Perfect love.	Full of fear.
Perfect peace.	Full of discord.
The immortal.	The mortal.
The living.	Dying.
The loving.	Hating.
Rest.	Unrest.
The incorruptible.	The corruptible.
The wheat.	The tares.
The sheep.	The goats.
Truth speaks to these,	To these Truth says,
"Unter thou into the joy of thy Lord."	"Depart from me, I never knew you."

That which Truth *never knew*, has *no truth in it*, is therefore falsehood.

All Truth belongs in the *Divine Nature*, and here we find, in the separation taking place within us, Peace, Perfection, Life, Health, Strength, and *all* Good, hence we declare these to be truth. *All untruth belongs* in the *claim of a mortal nature*, and here we find arrayed, discord, imperfection, sin, sickness and death, all evil.

In the Divine Nature, God, Spirit, Infinite Mind is seen as the Master sowing Good seed only; here is the "Wheat." In the claim of a mortal nature, man has fallen asleep to Truth, and his dreams, which seem *so real*, while he is in them, are of suffering, death, evil and darkness.

He begins to be aroused by the voice of Truth saying, (*Eph. 4:14*), "Awake, thou that sleepest, and arise from the dead, and Christ shall give thee light."

"It is high time to awake out of sleep, for now is our

salvation nearer than when we believed. The night is far spent, the *day is at hand.*"—*Rom. 13:11.*

The "deep sleep" that fell upon Adam, has held the race in dullness until this day. But it is written, "As in Adam *all* die, so in Christ shall *all* be made alive." Not in some far off Adam, any more than a far off Christ! In the ignorant thought *within us,* is belief of separation and death. Also in the consciousness of sonship within us, is knowledge of oneness and life eternal for all.

In this "sleep," the whole race have believed in separation from God, which means separation from Peace, from Life, from Spirit and Wisdom, from Strength and Wholeness. We have the "fruit" of that belief. It appears as *our* world of sin and suffering.

In the awaking, we begin to see the falseness of these universal, or race beliefs; we see there is no separation from God, no world of our own, no mind of our own, no life separate from God; no power, no presence, no knowledge but God Mind.

But, as when we awaken from a deep sleep, we do not in a moment throw off the spell of the sleep and its dream, so we do not at once and for all, give up that which has held us so long. We are not at first *wide awake*; sometimes we indulge in a little more sleep, and go back into our dream! But "morning" has come, the "day" has dawned, darkness is disappearing, and we *must* arise.

After we are fully aroused, we often smile at the absurdity of our dreams; sometimes we are so glad to know that they are *not true.* How much more satisfaction shall we feel when we "awake to righteousness," which is right thinking, "I shall be satisfied when I awake with thy likeness."—*Prov. 17:15.* When I *awake* to the *truth* of being in thy likeness, or of being Divine Nature.

What will help us to arouse quickly from our dream of error and evil? To cease to believe in error and evil, because we see Truth and Goodness as *All in all.* But we have seen the opposite so long it is hard to throw it off.

For this very reason we must not fall asleep again; the first awakening is the hardest; be persistent, be positive. What will help us to be positive?

First, "Bind the tares in bundles to burn them." We have bound them in bundles under Truth's directions. The race beliefs, the claim of a mortal nature, of something not born of God. All appearances of evil result from these beliefs, for we have seen how all sorrow and suffering follow in this train. How shall we "burn" these"? "Cast out the bond woman and her son." "The grace of God (which is light within) that bringeth salvation hath appeared to all men, *teaching* us that, *denying* ungodliness and worldly lusts, we should live soberly, righteously and godly in *this present* world."—*Titus 2:12.*

The surest way to become free from evil is to *deny* it a *place;* deny all that is ungodlike. We can do this when we know God is all. Begin and deny each claim separately. "There is no truth in the claim of a mortal nature. There is nothing that is not of God. There is no separation from God. There is, therefore, no world of sin, sickness, discord, or fear. "God hath not given us a spirit of fear."—*1 Tim. 1:7.* There is no death. There is no hate. There is no suffering in the world; for

There is no mind but Immortal Mind.

There is no power in any claim of evil.

There is no power in the false race beliefs.

There is no place for evil or error.

There is no self apart from God."

When we deny the race beliefs—the universal opinions about fear, trouble, sickness and death, which bind us, until by *Truth*, we see our freedom, we have handled the strongest claim of error there is, one of the largest "bundles."

Remember, error and evil are only claims, resulting from ignorance of God, and belief of separation; deny ignorance, it does not belong to Divine Mind, and Divine Mind is All-Presence.

Deny separation—there is none. All are in the One. While we have not *seen* God every where, we have *believed* in seeing something *not* God. This belief is that which must be "cast out," and is cast out by our denials; because as we deny, we cease to believe in it.

Jacob, in his sleep, saw a ladder reaching from heaven to earth. Angels ascended and descended. So in sleep have we believed in the visitation of "angels," but God's presence was at the other end of the ladder.

When "morning" came and "day" dawned to Jacob, he saw differently. "When Jacob *awaked* out of *his sleep* he said, Surely the Lord is *in this place*, and I knew it not. . . . *This* is none other but the house of God, and this is the gate of heaven."—*Gen. 28:16, 17.*

When the disciples questioned Jesus about their inability to heal a certain case, he said it was because of their *unbelief.* He added these words: "Howbeit this kind goeth not out, but by prayer and fasting." This is just as true to-day. We must fast and pray without ceasing.

Fasting in its inner sense, is the soul's denial of all the claims of sense; denying the old mortal idea of life and of self; that the Divine Idea may more fully possess our thoughts.

"The Lord is in the midst of thee, thine eye shall not see evil any more."

DENY THYSELF.

I have no *self* apart from God.

There is no Mind, Life, Power, or Substance, apart from God.

There is no Mind or Power of darkness, or evil.

There is no reality or power in fear.

"God hath not given us fear." There *is* no fear.

There is no evil. There is no death.

There is no cause of suffering or sorrow.

These *claims* are not found in the Source of All.

Man is not born of flesh.

Man does not inherit from flesh.

Man is not heir to ills of flesh.

There is no flesh, for *all* is Spirit.

I am not "conceived in sin," nor "shapen in iniquity."

God *only* is my Father, my Lifegiver, my Source.

I am not affected by universal beliefs of sin, evil and death.

There is no universal mortal mind.

I have no past outside of God.

I have no doubt, anxiety, or fear.

I have no uncertainty of Life.

I have no ignorance.

I am nothing of myself. I am all in God.

The *Truth* hath made me free.

PRAYER.

FASTING, in its spiritual sense, is breaking away from all that binds or limits. We may do this by ejection of past ideas which contain belief of *any opposite* to God.

"Is not this the fast which I have chosen: To *loose* the bands of wickedness, to *undo* the heavy burdens, to let the oppressed *go free*, and that ye *break every yoke?* . . . Then shall thy light break forth as the morning, and thy health spring forth speedily."—*Isa. 58:6, 8.*

When the light of true judgment has illumined our consciousness, we know how to fulfill this "fast."

"Ye cannot serve two Masters," Jesus said; Which is to say: Ye cannot acknowledge two powers. Because we have done so, we must now break the yoke of bondage to one or the other; shall we acknowledge the power of Spirit only? If so, we must free ourselves from the belief of bondage to the flesh. "There is no power but of God; no power but Spirit," may be our denial for this. Jesus said: "Now is the axe laid at the *root* of the tree, and every plant that my Father *hath not planted* shall be *rooted up.*"

Cause of evil and error must be struck at, not the outer effect. Cause of sickness and sorrow must be destroyed, and not just the appearance. Truth cuts *deep*, and roots out "Every plant which my Father hath not planted;" because Truth reveals that whatever the Father hath not planted, has *no reality, no cause;* this understanding *destroys* the *cause* of sin, sickness and death. There is no cause of evil; when we see this, a blow has been made at the *root*, which shall finally destroy the entire plant."—*Isa. 52:2, 5.*

To clear our garden of weeds, we clean them out root and all, for if we cut away only the tops we shall have an abundant crop again. To heal the sickness of the body is like cutting off the tops of our weeds, and leaving all the roots to put forth again in new growth.

Science goes always into Cause; and as there is but One Cause to go into, and that forever Good, it soon eliminates the *cause* of *evil*, seeing it has none! The only supposed cause of evil and suffering is the thought of separation from Good. There *is no* separation from God. Truth destroys *this* "cause."

Fasting is "casting down imaginations," or false images thought is holding. "And every high thing that exalteth itself against the knowledge of God: and bringing into captivity *every thought*, to the obedience of Christ."—*2 Cor. 10:5.*

That which sees things contrary to God is imagination. "And God saw that . . . every imagination of the thoughts of man's heart was only evil continually."—*Gen. 6:5.* This condition caused the "flood," and within each of us, the flood shall come, that shall destroy these imaginations. When the soul is flooded with the light of Truth and Love, "The world of the ungodly" perishes; the imagination that there is an ungodly world, is destroyed. Righteous thought—Noah, (*Gen. 7:1*), is separated from all unrighteousness, that ungodliness may be destroyed.

Fasting is "shutting the door" when thought enters into communion with All-Spirit. It shuts out every ·thing but Spirit, seeing that Spirit is all. Hence fasting *prepares the way* for prayer; it empties thought, making it ready for, or receptive to refilling. "Empty that he might fill me," expresses the idea of fasting and prayer.

Thought emptied of its own opinions and ideas, is cleansed, and prepared to be filled with Divine Idea.

Prayer is the complement of fasting. After the emptying must come the filling; after the rooting out, comes the re-sowing; after tearing down, we want to build; after fasting we must pray.

As a new idea of Truth dawns in our understanding, one of the first questions it stirs up is, How shall I pray? which shows that our prayer changes as our consciousness changes.

As Jesus opened the disciples' eyes to more Spiritual understanding, we hear them asking at once, "Lord, teach us how to pray."

As consciousness increases, prayer assumes new meaning, and the words of our childhood—the "milk" that belonged to babyhood—no longer satisfy our fuller grown thought.

To find a more helpful idea of prayer, which our new consciousness demands, we first must know what the purpose of prayer is.

Prayer cannot, and has never changed God. We read, in *Isaiah 51:9*, the prayer of Israel, calling upon God, to awake. "Awake, awake, put on strength, O arm of the Lord." This is the prayer of childhood, and the answer comes back, (*Isa. 52:1*), "Awake, awake, put on *thy strength*, O Zion." "Zion" needs to awake, not God.

As soon as we understand that the *All* is Everpresent, that we live in It, and that "All things are ours," we see that the purpose of prayer is not to bring anything to us, is not to induce the Divine to grant us, what it would otherwise not have given, but to *bring us* into a realization of the Fulness of Good, that is everywhere present, so that we may *accept* the Eternal gift of Love.

One says, "God has given all of Himself to each one. He has nothing more to give." And when Truth declares, "Before they call I will answer," it is as much as to say, everything is given them, before they ask for it. Asking does not then bring anything to us, but earnest seeking helps us to find and receive that which is always "at hand."

God's Omnipresence makes us sure of all good here and now, and when this consciousness is ours, prayer changes. We have no more pleading to do, but we desire only to have *our eyes opened*, to see what is here for us in Truth.

When Hagar wept and "Lifted up her voice," praying for water, that her son might live, "God *opened her eyes*, and she *saw* a well of water."—*Gen. 21:19*.

Prayer opens our eyes to see God's everpresent supply, and we see there is no lack. Because "Eye hath not *seen*," and "Ear hath not *heard*," we have been "hungry" and "thirsty" in the midst of full supply. "Prayer is not overcoming God's reluctance, it is *laying hold* of His Highest willingness."

In this understanding, Jesus' words come to us with clear meaning, "Therefore all things whatsoever ye ask and pray for, believe that ye *have received*, and ye shall have."—*Mark 11:24. (Rev. Ver.)*

No more pleading when our eyes and ears are opened to see and hear the good that is all around us—that is ours—as "Heirs of God."

If we pray as Jesus here directs, our petitions will be changed to thanksgiving, as we recognize that we "have received" all things!

Jesus' prayer at the tomb of Lazarus, before he had called upon him to come forth from the dead, should be ours in all that we desire: "Father, I thank Thee, that Thou *hast heard* me, and I know that Thou hearest me always."

It is also written: "If we *know that he heareth us*, we also *know* that we *have* the petitions that we desired of Him."—*1 Jno. 5:15*. When we know that He "heareth us always," we will joyfully declare this, as Jesus did, rather than plead, as of old: "*Hear* our prayer, good Lord." Our manner of praying will be, then, according to our understanding of God, and man's relation to God.

While we believe in God as a Great Personality, seated in some far off heaven, arbitrary in will and purpose, swayed by man's pleadings, moved by his desires, sending good gifts as a reward, withholding good as a punishment, we will send up our petitions and pleadings without cessation.

When we know God as Changeless Power and Presence, always Love, forever Good, Eternal Fulness, "Without shadow of turning," *filling full* heaven and earth; that the kingdom of All Good is within us; that this Infinite Good-Presence does not change, because it is always Perfection; does not make *special gifts*, but forever *gives all* to all; then we pray according to this knowledge.

We know that every good thing is ready and waiting for us to accept with loving gratitude; that in the "Son" we are heirs to this All-good, everpresent. We hear Spirit saying to Its Own Begotten in us: "Son, *all that I have is thine*"; and we answer: "All mine are thine, and all thine are mine." Blindness—ignorance only—has kept us from receiving all good; we have not *seen*.

It is written, (*Jer. 17:5-8*), "Cursed be the man that

trusteth in man and maketh flesh his arm"; that trusteth
in man's opinions; that believes in Life and Understanding apart from God.   "For he shall be like the heath in
the desert, and shall not *see when good cometh*. . . . .
Blessed is the man that trusteth in the Lord, . . . for
he shall be as a tree planted by the waters . . . and
shalt not *see when heat cometh*."

So we need not ask God to be near us; Good cannot
come any nearer than it always is ! Let us then seek to
realize how near God is. We will not ask for more life,
more strength, more health, to be given us; but will try
to appreciate and accept the changeless Life and
Strength, the perfect Health in which we live. "Shall
we plead for *more* at the open Fount, which already
pours forth more than we can" (or know how) "to receive"?—*S. and H.* What then shall we ask for? Only
that our eyes may be opened to see what eternally *is*.

Consciousness of God enables us to claim what is;
to recognize our Father's good gifts and good will. The
prayer then of a higher understanding is *recognition* of
Truth, and willing thanksgiving.

> "In happy childhood, at a father's call,
> Trusting we walk wherever He may lead.
> We say not: 'Father, do not let me fall
> Down this steep hill.' We *feel so safe*, that all
> We think is to enjoy his loving heed.
> We never plead: 'Do not forget, I pray,
> To give me food and drink enough to-day.'
> Why should we with a heavenly Father plead?"

In a better consciousness, the pleading of God's children, gives place to joyful recognition. Many, at this
point, call attention to the "Lord's Prayer," and ask, Is
not that full of petition? Granted that it is, we must remember that Jesus himself, admitted his restriction in
speaking, because of lack of understanding in his hear-

ers. - He must give the prayer which the consciousness of his hearers could receive. The Spirit of Truth is revealing the "many things" that Jesus could not then tell about; and clearer consciousness can receive them.

But we notice that in the Lord's Prayer there is *no* "*if.*" It seems that the greatest hindrance to answer of prayer, has been because of that little word "if," which Jesus never directed us to use. Webster defines "if" to mean, "In case that, or supposing that." Then "if" implies doubt, and doubting prayer is not answered. "He that wavereth is like a wave of the sea. . . . Let not that man think that he shall receive anything of the Lord."—*James 1:6, 7.*

Jesus indicated the need of perfect confidence when he said, "Whosoever shall *say* to this mountain, *Be thou* removed, and shall not doubt in his heart, but shall *believe* that *what he saith* comes to pass, he shall have it." Here we are authorized to speak positively, which we never do when we put an "if" in.

When we know that "The word which I speak is not mine, but the Father's," we will also know that it "Shall not return unto me void."

But one will say, "I pray, If it be thy will, because I am not sure whether it is God's will or not." In such a case, we had better at once enlighten ourselves about God's will; there is no excuse for not knowing it. As Paul says: "Be not foolish, but know what the will of the Lord is."—*Eph. 5:17.* (*Rev. Ver.*)

"The Lord *shall* preserve thee from all evil," (*Psl. 121:7*), is a statement in His Word, and makes plain God's will towards us. Again, it is told us clearly, in *Gal. 1:4,* "Who gave himself for our sins, that he might *deliver us* from this *present evil world, according* to the *will of God.*" One came to Jesus, saying: "Lord, *if* Thou *wilt,* thou *canst* make me clean." Not doubting his power—I know thou canst—but uncertain about his *willingness*. Jesus' answer to this one is the answer for all in such doubt, "*I will:* be thou clean." God is always more willing to give than we are to receive !

When we understand God's will, as Jesus did, how gladly will we say, "Not my will, but Thine," for as one says: "The 'I will' in Truth is God's will." This we see, when we know that the *One* is *All*; One Mind; One Intelligence; One Will.

Jesus said: "Abide in me"; be firm or fixed in consciousness of the One that I am, "And ye shall ask what *ye will*, and it shall be done unto you," for it is then the One Will. "It is God that worketh in me both *to will* and to do of His good pleasure," after I have given up all belief of separateness.

Jesus again said: "If ye ask *anything* in my name, I will do it"; does not say in these boundless promises, "I will do it if it is best for you," but simply, I will do it. Do what? "*Anything*" you wish, but seek it "*in my name.*" This is the secret. We may find everything in that wonderful Divine Name, *I am*, which is also Divine Nature. *In* the Divine Nature we have all things we desire: Peace, Health, Strength, All-good is there, and is ours in that Nature, which I am. We can feel no doubt, nor say an "if" when we understand asking "in his name."

"Open thy mouth *wide* and I will *fill* it."—*Psl. 81:10.* Make plenty of room to receive, the Divine sets no limit. If thought is half filled with belief of evil, it cannot be more than *half* filled with good. If thought is emptied of all belief of evil, it can be filled *full* of good.

"Prove me now, saith the Lord, if I will not open the *windows* of heaven (open your spiritual eyes to see) and

pour out a blessing that there shall not be room enough."
—*Mal. 3 :10.*

What we recive is not limited by the Giver, but by
our capacity to receive.

"When the poor widow applied to Elisha for aid, he
met her need by increasing the oil she had in the house;
and the limit of increase was set, not by the Giver of every good gift, not by Elisha, through whom the blessing
came, but by the widow who *measured for herself!* The
oil ran until it filled every vessel *she had set* to contain it!
And when there was not a vessel more, the oil stayed."

As one says, "our failure to receive comes from self
made limitations."

What shall we ask for? Jesus told us, when he said,
"Seek ye first the kingdom of heaven." And David gave
us the right idea of prayer when he declared, "*One* thing
have I desired of the Lord, that will I seek after; that I
may dwell in the house of the Lord forever."—*Psl. 27:4.*

The kindom of God is also God's house; David was
seeking the kingdom of God, or to *dwell* in God's presence. To become *conscious* of God's All-Presence is to
dwell in that Presence. If we declare God's Presence as
all, we help our thought to dwell in that consciousness —
to dwell in God's "House."

Jesus said (*Luke, 10:42*): "But *one* thing is needful."
This one thing is to *recognize* the everpresent God or
Good.

Can we concentrate our desires to "one thing?"
When we do, we shall find in that "one thing." whatever
we would ask for. It is His Holy Name or Nature; it is
His One Only Presence and Power, which we are to joyfully acknowledge and accept.

Our past praying, has been so mixed with doubt, because we have not seen God's will clearly, and could not

understand that the All-Good was ours before we began to pray, so we never felt *certain* of the answer! This need not discourage us, because when we know better, we shall pray better!

When Peter was imprisoned by Herod, we read that "Prayer was made without ceasing, of the church unto God for him." On the night of his delivery he went to a house where "Many were gathered together praying." Peter knocked at the door, and the maid, who knew Peter's voice, ran in to those praying, and "Told them how Peter stood before the gate." And they said unto her, "Thou art mad!" But she constantly affirmed that it was even so. "Then," said they, "it is his angel!" The need, just as truly now as then, is to have *more faith* in our prayers! And knowledge will give us that faith. In clearer understanding we will revise our form of prayer. Our old and well loved "Now I lay me," has new strength and meaning in its "new" form:

A CHILD'S PRAYER.

"Now I lay me down to sleep,
I *know* that God His child doth keep,
I *know* that God my life is nigh,
I *live* in Him, I cannot die.

God is my Health, I can't be sick,
God is my Strength, unfailing, quick.
God is my All, I know no fear,
Since Life, and Truth, and Love are here."

"Oh, Thou All-seeing, and All-knowing One,
Whom we call 'Father,' 'God,' 'Creator,'—to Thee
We pray, not as of old when ignorance of Thy laws
And Thee, did bid us supplicate, entreat,
Implore for things we most desired.
But in the higher understanding
With which our great Teacher bade us pray;
He who said: 'When thou prayest, *believe*
That things desired by thee, *are thine!*
For thy Father knoweth *all thy heart,*
And gives thee all good blessings, *e'er thy prayer
Is uttered'!* God is perfection, law itself,
And *He* no changing needs. But we, His children,
Heirs by birth and inheritance, have lived
So long *in doubt* of our estate, cannot receive;
Our spiritual ears, eyes and thoughts are silent;
   So *we the changing need.*
Now when we pray, we will not say:
'Dear Father, hear our prayer;' but *know*
That Thou *dost hear*, and answer!
We will not plead, 'Be near us,'
But *know* that space is *filled* by *Thee alone!*
And surely Thou art here as *everywhere.*
We will not *plead* that Spirit's power,
May us encompass and protect,
We *know* that spirit never leaves us day or night.
We'll let each breath, and thought, and word,
A *recognition* be, our lives be hid in Thee.
Content in Thee, we find our heaven *now.*
And *nothing* have to fear,
Since God is 'All in All,' and God is *good.*"

I AND MY FATHER ARE ONE.

One in Life, in Mind, in Idea, in Consciousness;
One in Truth, in Freedom, in Fulness, in Wisdom;
One in Strength, in Wholeness, in Peace, and Rest.

God, my Source, is Omnipresent, Omnipotent, Omniscient Life and Love.

I (my name, or my patient's name) express the Omnipresent, Omnipotent, Omniscient Life and Love.

I, (patient's name), the individual, express all the Truth of the Universal Divine Man.

The Universal says: I *am* Divine Man, one with God; one with Life, Truth, and Love.

The individual says: I *express* the Whole Truth of Divine Man; his Perfection, Peace, Wholeness, Ease, Understanding, Harmony, Goodness, and Love.

The Spirit of Love fills the universe of God.

I live in the full Power and Presence of Love.

Spirit fills all time and all places.

Every moment is brimming full of Life—Eternal and Changeless.

Because God is Life, I (patient's name) express life; because God is Wholeness, I express health; because God is Peace, I express peace and ease.

(After emptying thought by the denials given, fill it with these Divine affirmations).

GROWTH.

"FOR by thy words thou shalt be justified and, by thy words thou shalt be condemned."—*Matt. 12:37.*

Science turns about (converts) our thoughts from the outward to the inward; from the visible to the invisible; from appearances to righteous judgment; from the body to Spirit; from the word to Mind; from the fruit to the Vine; from effect to Cause. By thus looking beyond appearances, I can see by Divine Light, what I am.

Before I can judge righteously, and *appear* right, I must know what it is to *be* right.

The spoken word is, as Webster defines it: A sign or symbol of an idea in Mind. Every word spoken—which also signifies every *visible thing*—has an idea back of it, in which it originated. The idea is the unspoken word; the spoken word is the idea expressed. The idea is first, therefore is the power that is in the word. Hence all power is in Mind, and the word expresses that power.

In Divine Mind is the Eternal Idea of all things. "The word that was in the beginning with God, and was God." This word is complete in God, *before* it is *spoken forth;* for it is God's complete Idea, which is All-Good, All-Perfection, All-Truth. So when we speak the Word of Truth, we speak of *finished work*, that which is eternally done in God; hence our speaking does not *make* any truth, but it expresses, or brings forth, the Truth that *is*, and that was, *before* we spoke.

This explains many verses in the Bible, as *Gen. 2:4, 5*, "In the day that the Lord God made every plant of the field *before* it was *in* the *earth*, and every herb of the field, *before* it *grew.*" And again, in *Heb. 4:3*, "For we which have believed do enter into *rest.* . . . The works were *finished* from the foundation of the world"; or *Eph. 2:9*, "Not of works lest any man should boast."

> My Eternal Life is a finished fact.
> My Health is a finished fact.
> My Peace is a finished fact.

We can never in Truth assume that individually we have done anything; not even can we claim by *our* understanding, to have accomplished aught. *Divine* Understanding enlightens our thought to see that which is *eternally fiinished in Truth.* And as soon as we see it, we begin to think it, and to declare it: this is to be our work. Our part is to believe in the *finished* Truth of all things in God.

The Truth that thus presents itself to us, is God's Divine Idea; we have called it the Christ—always Full and Complete. We are to *believe in* this Fulness and Completeness of all things, and this helps us to understand that, which Jesus declares to be the "work" which God requires of each soul. *Jno. 6:29*, "This is the work of God, that ye *believe* on him whom He hath sent." We are to *believe* on, and to be positive about the finished work of God—the Divine that He hath sent into all.

Now, I desire to be good, where shall I begin? Shall I try to make myself good by *acting* good? This would be trying individually to make something, which is impossible. If I want a beautiful lilly, do I try to make the flower *first?* or do I plant deep out of sight, a lilly bulb, which in due time sends forth stems, out of which burst the blossom? All of us can plant a bulb and have a lilly. The bulb contains within it the perfect lilly; the flower is the result of the perfect life and substance that is in the bulb.

This bulb may represent to us our Divine Nature. The planting of it in mother earth, may remind us to see our Divine Nature implanted within the Whole Divine Life, the Mother, Father, God Source of all; Power in and through all; "Your life is hid with Christ in God."— *Col. 3:3.*

To understand my life buried with Truth in God, is to plant the bulb of my existence, the starting point of all outward expression of good.

The "stem" and "flower" represent to us this outward expression, put forth from within the bulb, *after it is buried.* When we look from the visible to the Invisible Life, from the act to the Actor, or Power of Action, Divine Life stirs up our souls, by pushing out Its own action, and the *result* comes into the visible *act* of goodness.

With faith in the bulb, and what it can do, we plant it, and *wait.* With faith in Divine Nature, and what it can do, we *believe in it,* and wait. "For we have need of patience that after we have *done the will,* we may receive the promise."

The Divine Soul is the budding out of the Spirit of Life, Truth, and Love. The Divine Body is the development of this bud into the perfect flower.

When thought is truly converted, it sees that we cannot *make* perfect lives, but we can *be* the Perfect Life in God, and thus let *it* put forth its perfection, peace, and beauty, into soul and body.

We cannot make good acts that are genuine; they must unfold from within good thoughts, which rest, or are positive in Good Being. All Truth must come from Source.

We cannot then make good health! There is just One Law of making or expressing anything.

We must go into Source and Cause, and *see* Good Health as an eternal fact—a finished Truth—then we *will believe* in good health only, and wait. By the law we have seen, this bud of good health, shall unfold into the perfect expression.

We cannot make the body well permanently, while thought is based upon ill-health as a truth. If we desire a well body, we must "Work as the Father works," which is to say we must recognize the Divine Law and method.

First, a well mind. As there is but One Mind, and that the Infinite, we can easily see that Mind is well! There is no Mind of disease.

Second, a well thought—and this comes naturally from a sound Mind.

Third, a well body—the sure result of a sound Mind and Thought.

"God hath not given us a Spirit of fear, but (God hath given us a Spirit) of love, and of power, and of a sound mind."—*2 Tim. 1:7.* Therefore claim, "I have a sound mind, a sound thought, and a well body." This is the way to look to God for our good health. Joyfully recognize "What God *hath* prepared" for us. My good health is finished in God, is waiting for me to *accept.*

This is the whole Law of expression, which means the law of growth. It is always from within, outward.

"Consider the lillies how they grow; they toil not, neither do they spin." "Which of you, by taking thought, can add one cubit unto his stature."—*Matt. 6:*

27, 28. These words contain such a wonderful secret :
the whole mystery of growth is wrapped up in them.

Toil not, labor not *to grow*. Growth is never pro-
moted in that way; busy thought never adds to your
stature, and yet thought was made to be busy, for
thought is the action of Mind !

It is natural to grow, and we grow without effort.
If we use thought as a cause of growth, we make a mistake; thought is only the *method* by which growth is accomplished; the impelling power is in Mind which moves
thought on to do its will. Thought is the servant, not
Master; the action, not the Actor; the expression, not
the Expressor.

Thought does not add to my stature, because I am
that I am, eternally. Thought may *see* what I am, and
seeing, declare it, The work of thought is not to make
me anything, but to continually express what I am.

"Their strength is to *sit still*." In the outer, be pas-
sive, but in the inner, to "sit still" is to be brimful of the
consciousness of Omnipotence ! Be positive.

"For thus saith the Lord . . . in returning and
rest shall ye be saved; in quiet and confidence shall be
your strength; and ye whole not."—*Isa. 30:7-15.*

"O, Jerusalem, . . . how often would I have
gathered thy children together, even as a hen gathereth
her chickens under her wings, and we would not."—*Matt.
23:37.*

"Ye will not come unto me that ye might have life."
—*Jno. 5:40.*

We cannot "sit still" in Life, in Truth, and in Love,
until we have come into Christ—come into knowledge of
being Divine. Then *I* rest in *Being*; I direct thoughts to
express the truth of my Being Divine, and the word, or
visible result of thought, will follow. Growth, then, is

not making myself *become* anything, it is becoming more and more conscious of what I am.

Because we have not recognized the truth of our Life and Being, thought has become filled with images of false being, which have obscured the true idea.   Our visible world rests under the shadow of such false belief; for it is an acknowledged fact, by many thinkers, that creation, or the visible, is mysteriously linked with man's thought.

"The student of nature observes, that all things in nature—the animals, mountains, seas, and stones—have a secret relation to man's thought and his life.   Nature gives him a *copy* of every mood and shade in his character and mind.   Every object he beholds is the mask of man.   Nature is the *immense shadow* of man."—*Victor Hugo.*

"The soul spreads *its own hue* over everything; the shroud or wedding garment of nature is woven in the loom of our own feelings."—*F. W. Robertson.*

The visible world *returns to us* our own opinions and beliefs.

"There is nothing either good or bad, but thinking makes it so."—*Shakespeare.*

"There is nothing unclean of itself; but to him that esteemeth a thing to be unclean, *to him* it is unclean."—*Paul.* His *thinking* makes it so to himself. We may as truly say, "There is nothing hurtful of itself, but to him that esteemeth a thing to be hurtful, to him it is hurtful."

To change our world, therefore, we must change our *thoughts* about it. "The things that *are seen* are temporal," because *our way* of seeing things shall change!

"The creation is on wheels, always passing into something else, streaming into something *higher;* everything undressing and stealing away from its old into new

forms. Thin or solid everything is in flight."—*Emerson*.
The outer is uplifted, as thought is enlightened by the
Truth, to see the true nature of all things.

"A pure inward life, may transform the outward
shape, and turn it by degrees, to the soul's essence, till all
be made immortal." "Be ye transformed by the renewing of your minds."

The whole world is to be transformed by the making
new of our thoughts of the world. When our belief of
the world is darkness, the shadow of sin, sickness and
death, or the absence of Purity, Health and Life seem to
be.

A little girl, when asked what made the daylight on
the earth truthfully replied: "The side of the earth that
is turned to the sun." But when asked again what makes
the night? naturally replied, "The side of the earth that
is turned *to darkness.*" There is no darkness for the earth
to turn towards! The darkness comes to the side of the
earth that is turned *away from the light.* And still more,
it is the earth's *own shadow* that creates darkness! If the
earth were transparent, the light of the sun would penetrate it through and through, and shine into it and beyond it everywhere. The *opaqueness* of the earth, throws
the shadow or darkness.

So the denseness of our thought, throws darkness
over our world; these dense thoughts stand between the
"Light that lighteth every man," and the world of *Truth*,
casting their shadow on all things. This is how "We
see through a glass darkly."

If our thoughts were clear, filled with light, then
we would see "Face to face"; or see everything as it is;
for the light would penetrate our thoughts through and
through, and shine upon all things.

These shadows cast from ignorant, dark thought

make our world *seem* enveloped in darkness, doubt, fear, error and evil; of this it is written: "For all that is in the world—the lust of the flesh, and the lust of the eyes, and the pride of life, is not of the Father, (not God's world,) but is of the world" (your own idea of the world). "And the world *passeth away*, and the lust thereof; but he that doeth the will of God abideth forever."—*1st Jno. 2:16,17.* It is descriptive of a mental state, opposed to spirituality, which shall pass away, as spirit is known to be all.

Of this "world" (our own ideas, in belief of separation) Jesus spoke when he said, "In the world ye shall have tribulation, but be of good cheer, I have overcome the world. Ye are not of the world, even as I am not of the world."

Our first, or infant ideas of things, shall pass away, as thought matures. "The first man is of the earth earthy"; this represents the earliest idea man has of himself. "But the second man is the Lord from heaven;" the latest, or last idea that man has of himself, when the "new" is "put on," "Created in rigteousness and true holiness." Man is to grow into this knowledge of himself, and the seed of such knowledge must be planted in the soil of Divine Mind, put forth through thought, and *last of all*, spoken out in word.

Hence to improve the world, we would not in Science begin our work with the world—not work to change the outer; "Not by might, nor by power, but by my Spirit, saith the Lord." Change the beliefs of thought into right knowledge; and this must be done, not by saying "I will," but by hearing the voice of Wisdom within saying "I am." Begin always with Divine Nature, let it reveal itself. This is what all creation is waiting for, as it is written: "The whole creation groaneth; *wait-*

ing for the *manifestation* of the sons of God."—*Rom. 8:22, 19.*

"Be still," is not slothfulness, but stilling mortal opinion, to let Divine Will have its full action. Be still, but *expectant*, wide awake, looking! "For to as many as *look for him*, he shall appear, without sin unto salvation." We receive what we look for, since that only have we "eyes" for. If we do not look for or expect good, we "shall not *see* when good cometh!" So of Health, of Life, and Strength, Peace and all good.

Two who had spent some time in India upon different missions, met, and each told his experience. The Missionary recounted his triumphs, and rejoiced in the number of converts; the hunter replied, "I do not believe there is a Christian in India, for I was there for months without *seeing* one."

Then the hunter told his story, and spoke of the number of bears he had seen and shot; the Minister replied, "I do not believe there is a bear in India, for I was there for years and never *saw* one."

We all *see* what we *look for*. As long as we say, "We must look for trials and sufferings, and sickness, and death, while we are in this world," we shall find just these. And we cannot but notice now, how busy people are looking for tribulations!

Let us consider a practical illustration of how to obtain good results by going into Source, rather than working with effect. I feel tired, my body rebels against further effort. I lie down, or lay the body down to rest it. I rise refreshed, but only for a time; soon again the body demands *rest;* it is right, it should have rest! Again I lay it down to rest; soon again it asks for rest, and it will continue to cry out for rest, until *we* learn how to give it true and permanent rest. How shall we do this? Go to where rest eternal is. "Come unto me, and rest." Enter into the Consciousness that *I am* Rest; my thought expresses the Rest that I am, and my body shows it forth—this is the only lasting rest; and the body will continually *demand* it, until we give it its own! The tired body then is a warning voice to us. "Give me my *true* rest."

Let us be willing to grow up into our Divine Nature in all things. Which means that in every place we recognize that the Divine is, and is the rewarder of all that seek it.

A STUDY OF THE TRINITY.

Three is the sign, or symbol, of completeness.
"Three in One," indicates the Complete One.
Mind is a Trinity in Unity, or is *complete* as
　　　　Mind, Idea, and Consciousness.

This is Infinite Mind, in Stillness and Fulness, but with all Power of action. It "creates," or manifests Itself in Its own likeness. Therefore we find the "Three in One" in all creation; and God-Mind includes the whole creation, and holds it in oneness with Itself.

In the Trinity we may say there is one, two, three.
The One is the Infinite Mind.
The Two is the *action* of the One Infinite.
The Three is the *result* of this action of the One.
The One is the Creator.
The two and three, or action and result, is the creation.

In the parable of the Vine, we find an illustration:
The One is the Vine.
The two and three are the branches and fruit; and Vine (Creator) includes and holds in oneness with itself, its branches and fruit (creation).

So there is but One in the universe—Mind, the Actor; and creation, the unfolding of Mind.

　　1.　Mind, the "Head."
　　2 and 3.　Creation, the "Body."　All One.

I. Infinite Mind.	1. Infinite Spirit.	1. The One.
2. *Its* Thought.	2. *Its* Soul.	2. Its Action.
3. *Its* Word.	3. *Its* Body.	3. Its Result.
1. Creator.	1. Infinite Cause.	1. The Vine.
2. Its Image.	2. Its Heavens.	2. Its Branches.
3. Its Likeness.	3. Its Earth.	3. Its Fruit.

"Upon the summit of each mountain-thought
Worship thou God; for Deity is seen
From every elevation of the soul."

"They shall not hurt nor destroy in all my holy
mountain; for the earth shall be full of the knowledge
of the Lord, as the waters cover the sea."—*Isa. 11:9.*

THE MOUNTAIN OF THE LORD.

"AND it shall come to pass in the last days, that the mountain of the Lord's house shall be established *in the top* of *the mountains*, and shall be exalted above the hills, and all nations shall flow into it. And many people shall go and say, Come ye, and let us go up to the Mountain of the Lord."—*Isa. 2:2.*

Mountain is the symbol of clear consciousness, or perfect spiritual realization. As we ascend a mountain our vision is extended; we rise above the earth—nearer heaven; we see more clearly. So does consciousness lift us above "earthiness," and give us plainer, broader vision. The "Mountain of the Lord's house," represents consciousness of God's presence, and the promise is, that in the "last days," or fuller light, the knowledge of God's presence shall be established above all other knowledge, and all others shall come into *it*.

This indicates plainly to us, that in due time, all things shall be brought into the Consciousness of Love, Life, and Truth. "For the knowledge of the Lord shall cover the earth, as the waters cover the sea." This Consciousness of Divinity as all in all, is now beginning to be our refuge. "Beautiful for situation is Mount Zion, God is known in her palaces for a refuge."—*Psl. 47:2, 3.* "Flee as a bird to your mountain, thou who are weary of sin." In perfect understanding, sin is not known. !

"O Zion, that bringeth good tidings, get thee up into

the high mountain." We know how Jesus went up into the mountain to pray; and it was in "an exceeding high mountain" that he met and conquered the strongest claims of the flesh! We need to be established in the highest consciousness, to be able to deny the allurements of sense, or appearances. In the Old Testament stories peculiar reference is made to mountains; and by finding the spiritual significance, most helpful truths are gleaned from the narratives.

"The ark rested upon the mountains," lifted up by the waters that had destroyed the "World of the ungodly." Our ark of safety finds its resting place in Divine Consciousness, borne upward upon the flood of light and Truth, that has destroyed *our* beliefs of darkness and error.

Moses went into the Mountain to receive the commands of the Lord. We likewise meet the Divine, face to face, when we rise into pure consciousness. John says that he was carried away in Spirit "To a great and high mountain," where he saw "The holy Jerusalem descending out of heaven from God."—*Rev. 21:10.* When in the Spirit we are lifted into "a great and high" consciousness, the same vision awaits us. We see in this high consciousness, heaven and earth as one heaven, and hear Truth saying, of this new heaven and earth, "And God shall wipe away all tears from their eyes, and there shall be no more death, neither sorrow, nor crying, neither shall there be any more pain, . . . and there shall be no more curse, . . . And there shall be no night there, . . . for the Lord God giveth them light."— *Rev. 21:4. 22:3, 5.* We cannot see this except from the height of pure Consciousness, even in "His holy mountain."

THE MOUNT OF CONSCIOUSNESS.

Each one stands now, somewhere on the "Mount of Consciousness." One may be lingering at the foot of this mount, where his vision is shut in, limited, Here his seeing is likely to be obscured by the mists of the valley; into this low spot, the sunlight reaches for only a few brief hours, the "shadows," therefore, fall long and deep. In the "valley" is the "shadow of death."—*Psl. 23:4.*

We hear this one praying for deliverance from these deep shadows and blinding mists. The answer comes, "Work out your own salvation. If you are seeing clouds and shadows, it proves that you are standing on low ground. Your only deliverance is, to *rise above* the *place* of mists and darkness. In the valley must ever be deep shadows and clouds, they belong to to the valley; but I have told you that 'There shall be no hurt in all my holy mountain.' Ascend, come *up;* and soon you will be lifted to where there are no shadows. 'Follow me.'"

Now the willing one, obedient to the guiding voice, begins to turn away from the valley, and to seek the mountain path; soon he sees a way that has been opened by the One who first ascended, and who now calls from the heights to all below him, "Come unto me"; "Come and be with me, where I am; come from the depths of your doubt and fear in the valley, to this summit of Light, where I stand. I have gone before and prepared a way for you. I wait to receive you here. I have overcome, by coming up over all doubts and darkness, and because I did this, you may also. The way is 'straight and narrow,' it leads *direct* to me."

This voice is heard even by those halting in the valley; and he who heeds, begins at once the ascent, although the way is not familiar at first.

But soon an exclamation of surprise is heard; as this

one advances in the new way, he cries, "How my view is broadening, how much freer I feel, how pure is the atmosphere becoming, how much clearer is the sunlight, how less dense the shadows! From where I now stand, I "see" what I never even conceived of while I was in the valley"!

From above a voice is heard, "And I, if I be lifted up, will draw all men unto me." And this ascending one, begins to understand the drawing power that is giving him strength to rise in consciousness.

So, all along, from the base to the summit of the mountain, are those who have left the valley, in obedience to the voice, and are attempting to attain the heights. Each speaks *his view*, from *his* standpoint, for the view changes with every upward step; and so we hear views given, differing according to the height reached in consciousnesss.

Some of these travelers move slowly, others rapidly. We see one who halts and hesitates, and learn that it is because he fears to go *too fast;* he wishes to be sure of every step of the way, before he takes it; he is so occupied with his own thoughts and beliefs, that he hears not clearly the voice that says "come," and feels uncertain as to just the direction from which it speaks. In his confusion he is sometimes led to believe that he must not try to rise higher, and then he halts. He does not realize that by going on up, his seeing will be clearer, and he will draw nearer to the voice that calls him, for it comes from the very summit of the mountain.

Another progress, slowly, as if burdened. We find that this one is trying to carry with him up the mountain, a remembrance of the "clouds and shadows" he has seen in the valley! He is so engrossed with trying to hold on to these memories, that he cannot hear the voice above saying, "Thy sins and thy iniquities, will *I* remember no more." He sighing says, "Whom the Lord loveth he chasteneth." He does not realize that the chastening means the purifying from all doubts and clouds, and an uplifting into Light! He does not know that all the "Scourging" comes in the clouds of the valley, because Love would draw us above them. "To him that overcometh (which is, 'cometh up over') will I grant to sit with me in my throne."—*Rev. 3:21*. This one does not "*Forget* the things that are being left behind," though it is written, "Remember ye not the former things, neither consider the things of old."—*Isa. 43:18*. So his progress in consciousness is hindered.

We meet another steadily pressing upward, and we hear him joyfully singing, "I will look unto the *hills* whence cometh my help. Who shall dwell in thy holy hill? He that walketh *uprightly*. I have set the Lord *always* before me. I shall not be moved. Thou wilt show me the path of life; in thy presence is fulness of joy," and we notice as these words are uttered, that the upward progress of this one, is rapid and easy; we remember it is written, "The joy of the Lord shall be your strength." And all who catch the echo of this rejoicing one, are strengthened to push on.

As we go higher, we see that all the other hills and moutains begin to disappear, as we are being exalted above them. All the hills of difficulty, which once arose so threateningly above us, now seem to be leveled, when looked *down* upon from this highest of mountains. Also as we look, the very valley we left is lifted up, and is seen no more as a valley! Now is the prophesy of Isaiah understood, "Every valley shall be exalted and every mountain and hill shall be made low."—*Isa. 40:4*. Fulfilled when the soul has reached the heights of Pure Consciousness, or the Consciousness of Purity filling all. "To the pure, all things are pure." This is the summit of the Mount, the Christ-consciousness towards which each soul on the Mount has been pressing, from the "beginning."

One says, "To get *above* the clouds you must ascend the mountain; so with the soul; it must rise to where it is lighted by Supreme Truth, before the mists of error and ignorance vanish."

"Behold the day of the Lord cometh, and it shall not be clear in some places, and dark in other places of the world, but it shall be *one day* which shall be known to the Lord."—*Zech. 14:1, 6, 7.* (Margin).

"There shall be one fold, one shepherd."

THE LAW OF HEREDITY.

In the second commandment it is written: "Visiting the iniquity of the fathers upon the children unto the third and fourth generation of them that hate me; and showing mercy unto thousands of them that love me and keep my commandments."

Upon these words, the universal belief in heredity is based. Even Christians claim its threat, of the visiting of iniquity upon the children of the Fathers that *hate me!* They claim for their children the inheritance of an evil habit, or a weak body from some ancestor, even though for generations back they have been God-loving people. They entirely forget that the assertion is, that the sins of iniquity shall be visited upon those that "*hate* me," but mercy is shown to "Those that love me." Certainly, Christians should insist upon freedom from heredity by this very second commandment.

To love God is to be conscious of God. Hate is the

opposite of Love; hence to hate God, is to be unconscious of God. Whenever we see evil, or see the absence of Good, we, in a sense, "hate" God, for we cannot see any absence of God, without being unconscious of God! Where we see absence, God is; therefore, to see evil, is to be *unconscious* of God's all presence, and this is to "hate" God.

In this understanding we can see the truth contained in the words above quoted.

"Visiting the iniquity of the fathers upon the children . . . of them that are unconscious of me; but showing mercy unto them that are conscious of me." To believe that man inherits any evil, is indeed an indication that thought is unconscious of Truth and Good; hence "The Truth shall make you free," for to become conscious of the Truth of Good only, is to be free in thought, from belief of evil inheritance.

In Ezekiel, eighteenth chapter, we read, long after the commandments had been given: "What mean ye by using this proverb, . . . saying, The fathers have eaten sour grapes, and the children's teeth have been set on edge? As I live, saith the Lord, ye shall not have occasion any more to use this proverb in Israel. The son shall not bear the iniquity of the father, neither shall the father bear the iniquity of the son," etc.

Later on, when Jesus spoke from still more perfect understanding, we hear him say, and now know his meaning: "Call no man on the earth your father; for one is your Father, even God." This forever settles the question! Man is child of God only; his Father is the Infinite Spirit of Perfection and Peace; now does he know what his inheritance is; and knowing, he claims it; and claiming, he possesses it, for it is his for the knowing. Therefore, in the Light of true Knowledge we say: Infinite Mind is the Only Source or Cause. I am in that Source eternally, and am of its Perfect Changeless Nature.

I am born of Spirit only, and am Spirit. This is my new birth, or new consciousness of birth. My inheritance is goodness and perfection in mind, thought, and body. I was made *whole*.

There is no source, or cause, of disease, weakness, or lack of any kind. I am eternally of Divine nature, and am filled full of all Truth from my Source.

WHAT I AM NOT.

God, or Good, is in everything.

There is nothing to be afraid of.

I am not afraid of any kind of weather.

I am not afraid of rain or wind.

I am not affected by cloud or sunshine.

I am not affected by anything *external.*

I am not afraid of anything I do.

I am not afraid of anything I eat.

I do not believe there is anything to hurt me.

I do not believe in two Minds or two Powers.

I do not believe in two Substances.

I am not bound by universal beliefs of fear and evil.

I am not influenced by individual claims of fear or evil,

I am free.

> "The value of a thought cannot be told.
> He lives most who thinks most.
> It is much less what we do, than
> What we think, that fits us for the future."
>
> *—Festus.*

"Christian experiences are not the work of magic, but come under the law of Cause and effect. Joy is as much a matter of Cause and effect, as pain. There is no mystery about Happiness whatever. Put in the ingredients and it must come out. All fruits *grow*, whether in the soil, or in the soul. Spend the time you have spent in sighing for fruits, in fulfilling the conditions of their growth. We have hitherto paid immense attention to *effects*. Henceforth let us deal with Causes.

Do not imagine that you have got these things because you know how to get them. As well try to feed upon a cookery book. What more need I add but this: *test the method by experiment*."—*Drummond.*

CONCLUSION.

"THERE is no new thing under the sun."—*Solomon.*
All Truth is Eternal; but man illumined by the increasing light of Spirit within, progresses in *consciousness*, and perceives Truth more and more dis-
tinctly; he is on his way to the "perfect day"; that is, to
perfect understanding.

One says: "Man is on his way to God, not by mere
lapse of time, but through various stages of illumination."
Man comes to God, by seeing God more and more clearly.

"Open Thou mine eyes, that I may behold wondrous
things out of thy law."—*Psl. 119:18.*

When Gehazi, the servant of Elisha, saw the city en-
compassed by the enemy, he said to Elisha: "Alas my
master, what shall we do"? "And Elisha prayed and
said: Lord, I pray thee *open his eyes* that he may *see;*
and behold the mountain was full of the horses and chariots of fire round about Elisha" As soon as his eyes
were opened, he saw the truth of Divine protection.

What were these "horses and chariots round about
Elisha"? We read, in *Psl. 68:17,* "The chariots of the
Lord are twenty thousand, even many thousands of
angels; the Lord is among them."

"The angel of the Lord encampeth round about them
that fear (or acknowledge) him and delivereth them."—
Psl. 34:7. Angels are Divine Thoughts: whisperings of
Truth and Love in the soul. These tell us of the Omnipresent Power of Good, and deliver us from all fear.

When our eyes are opened to see, we too are made conscious of the Divine that surrounds us, and can say, "I will fear no evil, for Thou art with me."

"Because thou hast made the Lord thy habitation," Because thou hast seen the Divine as thy dwelling place. "There shall no evil befall thee, nor any plague come nigh thy *dwelling*." Certainly not, for neither evil nor plague can come near to God. "For He shall give His angels charge over thee, to keep thee. . . They shall bear thee up, lest thou dash thy foot against a stone."—*Psl. 91:9:12.*

May we not trust in this, when we come to the rough, steep places in life's journey, that just "at hand" is the "chariot of the Lord," to bear us *up* above all hardship; that if we enter into Divine thinking, or thinking of the Divine Presence, All in all, nothing can be "hard" to us?

Let us not wait, however, until confronted by appearances that claim to be evil, before we establish our thoughts in Divine Consciousness. Begin at once, and continually try to see Divinity always at hand, wi:hin you; deny all other presence, power, or knowledge, a place. Do this while all seems well; then are you fortified when you see the "enemy all around."

We know that when a train approaches a tunnel, the lamps are all lighted while the train is still in daylight; then when it plunges into the darkness of the tunnel, it is all *light within*. If the lighting of the car were left to be done *after* the train had entered the tunnel, there would be much confusion, for it is too dark to see even how to make a light !

So we find many who have made just this mistake, and feel discouraged because in the darkness they could not find their light; in sickness they tried, but could not find their health!

We should carry our health, our light, our peace, always *burning* within us; and if we suddenly rush into a claim of sickness, it is all health within. If we plunge without warning into discord, it is all peace within.

If the within is fixed in health and peace, the without will soon be restored to harmony.

We need but to know the truth to be free, because we *are* free already from every mortal claim, and we only need to know it. "Open my eyes to see the Infinite Truth," is our prayer; and the answer comes, "Say to them that are of a fearful heart, fear not: the eyes of the blind *shall* be opened, and the ears of the deaf shall be unstopped. *Then* shall the lame man leap as the hart, and the tongue of the dumb sing. They shall obtain joy and gladness, and sorrow and sighing shall flee away."— *Isa. 35:4-10.*

How much we are able to "see," depends upon the height we have reached in Consciousness. A new understanding is our need, and not a new thing. "There *is* no new thing."

One says: "Our measure of Consciousness is our measure of life"; which is to say that we have all the life we are conscious of; and as truly may we say, we have all the good we are conscious of; our health is measured by our consciousness of Health; our strength, by our consciousness of Strength; our rest, by our consciousness of Rest.

Our Life, Health, Strength, Goodness, and Rest are limitless—we have all that we know how to claim.

To-day a deep and new idea of Truth is dawning in our consciousness; it does not appeal to material sense, for it is the Spirit of Truth that is leading us into this new consciousness, and as we read, "The natural man receiveth not the things of the Spirit of God, for they are foolishness unto him; neither can he know them, because they are *spiritually* discerned."—*1 Cor. 2:14.*

"The world, weary and disappointed, is wooed to listen to the more excellent way, which promises better results."

If we have worked a long problem in mathematics, and at the end find a mistake in our answer, how do we correct it? Are we willing to change the *figures* in our *result*, without going back over our work to see where the mistake began? Would a teacher allow a pupil to correct his mistake in that way, by simply changing his figures in the *answer?* Never! The scholar must learn *what* his mistake was, that in future he may, with better understanding, work more correctly, and be sure of correct results.

All our conditions of life, may be likened to the worked out example in mathematics. There is a Principle of Life, back of all examples in the visible, to be understood and demonstrated in living. We learn the Principle; the First Cause—the Source of every visible thing; we find that from this starting point, which is Infinite Mind, all things are brought forth. Our thought recognizes the Way and the Truth to be followed in its working, or reasoning. All things that come from this First Cause, or Source, must *agree* with It in nature; must be like It; must express Its Truth, Light, Goodness, Peace, and Wholeness. Our living, which includes all our conditions, should be an example, or proof, of its Source and Cause: for "The fruit of *Spirit* (of Principle, Mind, or Infinite Cause) is in all goodness," etc. Such would be a *perfect example* of Life. Complete, it is

Perfect Mind, as Cause;

Perfect Thought, and } as effect, for result,
Perfect Body,

We have found a Cause, or Principle, and know that when we rightly understand it, and work in accord with its Truth, by thinking rightly of the Life and Peace it contains for all, we shall have in all our *couditions*, rightness, peace, love, health, etc.

But now we are finding in our examples, conditions of not good, not peace, not health ! Without much consideration of the *right* way, we have tried to fix up this incorrect example by *changing its figures!* We have taken the sick body, which is one wrong figure, and tried to make it a well body by working to change the outer. This is just like changing our result in mathematics by altering the figures in the *answer*.

We call this, in school children, a dishonest method. I look on some other little girl's paper, who always gets her answers right, and I see I have gotten nine as an answer, and it ought to be ten. I just erase the nine and put ten in its place. Have I been helped by this? Only temporarily. I have been carried over a hard place.

So I may patch up the sick body for the time, but have gained nothing until I learn the mistake that produced the sick body, and find the antidote for all such conditions, in Divine Source.

To understand true healing, then, is to know, as exactly as in mathematics, what the *Principle of Health* is; what its law of demonstration, in order that I may always express this true condition.

"With all things, a right beginning is essential to a correct ending." It is then all important to know and understand the source of all things. One says: "To hold a false idea of God is to worship a false God." And to be ignorant of the True and Only Source, is to misunderstand our Life, and all its conditions. To know any, thing about our lives we must go into the Source of Life; to understand our health and strength and peace, we must go into the Source of Health, Strength and Peace, and *work it out* from there!

If then, "figures" or conditions appear in our answer to the "problem of Life," that do not harmonize with the Principle of Life, in goodness and peace, we may conclude that our work is wrong somewhere, and our wisest course is to do just as an honest scholar in mathematics does, erase our work and begin all over again.

It seems hard to some, that after having been religious all their lives, they are made to begin so far back, when they turn to Divine Science! But they come with anxious minds and sick bodies, which often have grown rebellious against former methods, and refuse to be improved thereby; so that they *must* have a better way, and in their earnest desire, they submit to the new method.

They are carried at once to the *Beginning* of all things, are shown the True and Eternal Nature of their own soul and body, in changeless Being or Spirit; are persuaded to rub out their past work, or method of reasoning from appearances, to go into Invisible Source, where all Good has its Beginning, and to bring forth by Divine Law or method, from Mind, through thought, into visible things, the Perfection and Truth of Divinity.

This is Divine Science. An exact knowledge of Being Divine; or Being perfect as Source is, in Mind, thought, and body; perfect in Strength, in Health; complete in Love and Truth and Life.

This is the true condition of the I am that I am, and I learn that as I think truly of the *I am*, knowing that "I and my Father are one"—one in Life, in Mind, in Idea, and Consciousness; one in Substance, one in Spirit or Being, as I *think* of this, beholding the glory of the *One Only I Am*, I must become individually in Its *image*, and express Its Omnipresent, Omnipotent, Life, and Goodness.

As I think in my heart, I shall manifest in my world, —this is the law. If I think holiness, my world will be holy—whole—complete. If I think not of holiness, my world will lack.

If I believe not in the unity of all things with Source, I see separation from God, and consequently a world *lacking* Ease, Light, Truth, and Love; it is the shadow of my own thought, and the wrong "figures" in the living example, all come from this.

The remedy is to enlighten thought, show it the One that is All and in All. "If thine eye be single, thy whole body shall be full of light." If my thought sees but One and that all light, then must my body be "full of light."

When we turn to the Infinite Source, we find It is Light—All that comes from Light is Light. We find It is Love, and all that comes from Love is Love. We find It is Mind or Spirit, and "That which is born of Spirit, is Spirit." It is Strength, Life, Health, and All Good; that which comes from It, is likewise Strength, Life, Health, and All Good.

If in any living thing there is a lack of Life, Intelligence, Strength, Wholeness, Peace and Good, these are the wrong "figures," because they give no representation of the Source, or Principle of Truth.

If the Good made all things and made them good, as the Word declares, and if without Good "Was nothing made that was made," then every true thing is good, and all that seems not good, is a false result from a false reasoning, or thinking.

Evil is not of God, therefore has no Source or Cause

in Truth.   Our mistakes put it there, our right knowledge will wash it out.

To Spiritual Being and Consciousness, there is no darkness, no error, no pain or disease, no evil. I am spiritual consciousness in Divine Mind, and I know the Divine and Perfect Idea of all things. This knowledge is the Light of my Spirit within me, which judges righteous judgment.

It separates from me, all claims of *Being* weak, erring, sinful, sick and dying. *It* says to these claims, "You are no part of the Divine Me. Depart from me into everlasting fire." The Light within becomes the consuming fire to all error.

We have let good and evil, Truth and error, Life and death, Peace and discord, Health and sickness, share our faith.   Now we refuse to do so! We *deny* the *truth* of evil appearances; because we do not find cause for them in the One Source, the One Life, the One Mind, the One Truth, we reject them; this is erasing our old wrong example, in order to write new and truer figures.

We find that by denials, our thought is freed from faith or belief in the power and presence of evil, or of anything not Good, and we are made ready to think wholly upon God as Omnipresent, Omnipotent, Omniscient Truth.

We can make these denials even in the face of appearances, when we have received clearly the Divine Truth, called the statement of Being: "*All* is Infinite Mind and Its manifestation," which means, that Infinite Mind with Its thought and word, Infinite Spirit with Its soul and body, Infinite Source with Its *image* and *likeness*, is all there is in the universe.   Or, as another states the same truth, "God, and God manifest is *all there is.*"

The same is declared by Paul in these words: "God is All and in all."

"Since God is *All*, there is no room for any opposite."—*S. and H.*

"To see the Divine Nature as *filling all*, is the destruction of every opposite claim."

One says, that all our trouble comes from the use of two little words, "mine" and "thine." These certainly admit a claim of separation When we learn to speak the "I am" in consciousness of oneness, we will know how to say with Jesus, "All thine are mine, and all mine are thine."

It has been written in one of the sacred books, "This is the great enemy, the *my*-ness in me." My thought of separation from God and from my fellow being, causes all belief of enmity.

Let us *deny* separateness, and declare oneness. The Great Source of Life and Light, pushes Itself into expression, just as the sun sheds its light in all directions. God's expression is man, and as the rays of light are forever joined to their Source, and shine by its light, not as separate rays, but blended into *one body* of light, so man is always united with his Source, and lives its Life, and is one Mind, soul, and body, with all expressions of Life.

Christ— Divine Nature—is the Head, the Foundation, the Beginning of all things. And all things are the "body" of Christ—the form of Divine Nature. As such, let us receive all things, as being in the nature of the Divine, whose Presence and Power, whose Light and Knowledge is *All*, and embraces all.

One Substance is the Substance of all things. There is no hurt for us in anything. Every breeze that blows, whispers of good; every thing that moves, tells of Divine Life and Presence. We have nothing to fear, therefore, "whether we eat or drink, or whatever we do, do all for the glory of God."

> "May not the lofty mountains and the hills
> Be voice of God? His song the gentle flowers,
> His chant the stars' procession; and, alas !
> His only sigh these human hearts of ours."

In full consciousness, there shall be no more pain or crying, for former idea of things is passed away. "Behold, all things are new.

WHAT I AM.

"God worketh through me to will and to do of His good pleasure." "In Him I live, move, and have my Being."

I am Life within Eternal Life.

I am Substance within the Eternal Substance.

I am Strength within the Infinite Strength.

I am Mind within the Divine Mind.

I am Idea within the Divine Idea.

I am Consciousness within Divine Consciousness.

I am Truth. I am Freedom. I am Fulness. I am that I am.

My life is complete now. I am eternally perfect.

My Health is a finished fact.

My Freedom is a changeless reality.

My Strength is Omnipotence.

My Understanding is Omniscience.

I now accept my always Perfect Health, my Changeless Freedom, my Unlimited Strength, my Divine Understanding and my Spiritual Substance from Thee, my Source.

"All souls shall be in God, and shall be God, and nothing but God be."—*Festus*.

SOME FINAL WORDS.

We learn, then, in Science, the futility of trying to better conditions, by working to change the *outer*, without reaching the inner Cause.

One has said, that although our streets were swept and kept as clean as the streets of heaven, and man's *thoughts* remained the same, every known disease would be repeated within a generation!

The outer is not a cause of anything; all cause is invisible; the visible is the effect, or result, of a cause.

To work scientifically, and this means to work with certain knowledge, and to be *certain* of results, we must *begin* with Source and Cause.

In Divine Science, we accept that the Source of all things is Divinity; that all Cause is Divine Mind. We follow the method of Divine Mind in expressing Itself, and know that Its first expression, or activity, is Divine Thought, and that the result of Divine Thought is Divine Word, or Body. As this Divine Mind is Omnipresent, and Its expression is always with It, we have *everywhere* the Divine, with Its image and likeness; Its expression and manifestation; Its thought and word; Its soul and body.

We do not pretend to *bring out* the expression and manifestation of Divine Mind into the visible, but we go into the Source and *follow* It out; see that it does *fill all* with Its perfect Presence, Invisible and visible.

As soon as we are willing to see the Omnipresence, Omnipotence, and Omniscience of Divine Mind, our "Whole body shall be *full* of light," for the visible will be seen in its true relation to the Invisible; it will be known as the result, or fruit, of Invisible Cause, which is Light. As soon as we know the Truth, we shall begin to be freed from all false ideas about the visible.

We look to *Source* only to find the *Truth* of things; for that which is in Source is all reality. We look upon "disease; immediately we ask, Has it a place in Source and Cause? No; Divine Mind is Perfect Ease, and can therefore, *as Source of all,* send forth only *ease.* Disease (of any kind) has no existence in Source; it has no place in Mind, hence no place in "thought," and no place in "body"; for thought and body, are image and likeness, expression and manifestation of Divine Mind, their Source.

There is, therefore, no truth in the *claim* of disease, no cause for disease. There is no disease in the world of God, or in the expression and manifestation of God.

We find that these *denials* of any opposite to God, or Good; any opposite to Ease, or Life, cleanse thought of its belief in fear and evil, and prepare it to believe only in God. Moreover, we have learned that as this change takes place in thought, appearances change; sickness, sorrow, and pain, fear, hate, and all discord, disappear. Then we know that there is no opposite to Good except in *our thought*, and when its belief is destroyed, the Cause or root of evil is touched, and the whole outgrowth of that belief begins to wither and die! Seeing but One Cause, and that All-Good, we can say, There is *no cause* for evil, and its appearances begin to go.

One says, "Regeneration means work." If we receive from these studies in Divine Science, only a beautiful *theory*, we have gained but little. Unless we put into practice, according to the rules given, its Divine Principle—meeting every condition in life with true judgment, by letting Divine Truth as seen in Source, settle every question for us; by daily *cleansing* thought of mortal claims—universal and individual, knowing that there is no mortal *Being*, the Only Being is the Divine; no mortal mind with its opinions, the Only Mind is the Immortal— therefore denying the claims of mortality any place; then stating or affirming the Truth of the I am until we are *sure* of what I am—unless we do this regularly and earnestly, we shall never know the freedom that is ours in Truth, of which these studies bear witness.

"He that willeth to do the will, shall know of the doctrine."—*Rev. Ver.*

"Let each man think himself an act of God,
His mind a thought, his life a breath of God,
And let each try by great thoughts and good deeds,
To show the most of heaven he hath in him."

REALIZATION FOR HEALTH.

All Reality is in God and like God. There is no re‾ality in darkness, doubt, fear, or evil.

I am that I am, for my Life is in God, my Being; my Strength is in God; my Health is in God; my Understanding and Wisdom is in God; therefore, my Life is Divine and Perfect; my Strength can never fail; my Health is always the same; my Understanding is complete.

I am expression of Perfect Life and Good, and I am kept by Divine Power, forever in the Truth.

I can never be separated from Truth, Life, and Love. I can never be out of Health, out of Peace, or out of Light. There is no darkness; there is no doubt or anxiety about anything; God is always my Light.

There is no disease in God. There is no truth in the world's claim of disease and death—such a thought has no reality. God is the Only Mind; there is no Mind of error, evil, or suffering. There is no *place* for error, disease, or pain, for God fills all.

There is no truth at all in the claim of sin or sickness; we cannot find these in the Source of all, and only that which is contained in Source is true. All Truth is in God.

That which is born of God, is the image of God, and cannot have any sickness or discord in it. The Divine *fills* all, hence, there is no place for pain or disease in my mind, my thought, or my body. I have no belief in pain. I am the Mind that knows all Peace. In Truth I am now *free* from every claim of ignorance, or error, for these are not to be found in God, and I am in God.

HOW TO REALIZE ILLUMINATION, OR UNDERSTANDING.

First, realize what I am.

I am Strength and Understanding. I am Light. I am that I am. I am Mind, I am Idea, I am Consciousness. I am all Wisdom within myself, for my *self* is God's Divine Idea.

There is no lack in the universe. God fills it all. There is no need of anything. There is no ignorance. Mind has no lack in It, and All is Mind.

There is no Mind of darkness or misunderstanding— no Mind of fear or error.

There is no fear. There is no cause of fear. There is nothing to be afraid of.

Light fills all—for Light is God.

Understanding is all in all.

I live, move and have my being in Light. I express perfect understanding.

I am Light, in Mind, in thought, and in body. I am all Light. I am complete. I am satisfied now.

I am filled full of the Fulness that filleth all. Life, Truth, Light, Love, and Understanding, are all mine in God.